CROUCHFIELD:

A HISTORY OF THE HERTS TRAINING SCHOOL

1857-1982

by Dorothy Abel Smith

Including some recollections by
those who knew the school.

**CROUCHFIELD: A HISTORY OF THE HERTS TRAINING SCHOOL
1857-1982**

Copyright © Dorothy Abel Smith, 2007

ISBN: 978 1 903607 85 5

All rights reserved.

Published by:

Able Publishing
13 Station Road
Knebworth
Hertfordshire SG3 6AP

www.ablepublishing.co.uk

I felt honoured to be invited to write a foreword to this fascinating book. The history of the Herts Training School, that in 1971 became the Crouchfield Community School, offers an insight into several different, but important, aspects of our society. The philanthropy, one hundred and fifty years ago, that brought the school into being has endured beyond the closure of the school with the creation of the Crouchfield Trust. Our society continues to benefit greatly from its long history of charitable giving by so many and by the innovation of organisations like Crouchfield. Moreover, the history of the school provides a rich insight into the social norms of succeeding generations and their response to the needs of delinquent young people. Significantly the material, so skilfully assembled by the author, ought to cause us to pause to reflect on past achievements and question whether we have yet devised the mechanisms to ensure a good prospect for each young person coming into the care of the state. Have subsequent changes been informed by fashion, finance or substance? Are the outcomes for delinquent young people better today than in times past?

A key feature of the school was the stability of the Headmasters and the Managers. They acted with care and imagination to the changing needs of the young people placed in their care. For most of the boys this was their first time away from their familiar surroundings and for many it became a life changing experience for good or ill. Most of the young people sent to the school were from impoverished inner city areas. The setting into which they were placed could hardly have been more different from their home circumstances. At Crouchfield their needs for education and training were certainly addressed. This book is so much more than a commentary on land and buildings. Rather it invites us to dwell on what we might learn from the experience of work with generations of young people who need help in being diverted from crime by becoming more fulfilled and successful members of the community.

I am delighted to commend this informative book and hope it will be well used in the best interests of young people with special needs.

The Lord Laming CBE DL
House of Lords, London

i

INTRODUCTION

In March 1982 the Herts Training School for Boys at Chapmore End closed its doors after 125 years. The buildings, in the fertile Rib Valley, lying in the Parish of Bengeo and on the B158 road from Hertford to Wadesmill were well hidden by trees and probably many people passing that way were unaware that a remarkable school was situated there and even more unaware of its interesting history.

A Reformatory School for Juvenile Offenders was founded there in 1857 and over the years saw many changes. On the School's closure by Hertfordshire County Council, the entire site was sold and the buildings developed. Today a large number of houses and flats, some converted from the former buildings, stand on old Crouchfield Farm.

County Hall and Hertford Museum often have enquiries from people who wish to know something about the school and its past, especially from those who live at Crouchfield now. This short story, written exactly 150 years since the founding, is intended as an informal record of the school and its history and includes recollections of those who knew the place. My father, Thomas Abel Smith devoted much of his time to the school from 1938-1973 serving on the management committee and latterly as Chairman; and I, as a descendant of the founders, am delighted to research the past.

I am grateful to Hertford Museum for the idea, the County Archivist and her staff at Hertfordshire Archives and Local Studies (HALS) for giving me access to the School Records and members of the Hertford Oral History Group for encouragement and use of their cassette tapes.

I am especially indebted to Lord Laming who has generously given me his time and his knowledge of Crouchfield in the 1970s and has written the Foreword.

None of the more recent history could have been achieved without the help of Mrs Paddy Harding, Geoffrey Mercer, the late Brian Coates, Dennis Buzzard, Anthony Joshua, Mr and Mrs Geoff Garton, John Bing and the many others who have provided vivid memories of the school and loaned illustrations. I appreciate their enthusiasm and thank them all.

I would also like to thank Michael Thornton for reading the draft text and Able Publishing for their assistance in preparing and printing the book.

During this research into the past and by speaking to people who have been associated with the Herts Training School, I have gained the greatest admiration and respect for their determination and commitment so I dedicate this small history to their memory.

Dorothy Abel Smith, 2007

'Let the past serve the present'
Chinese saying

Abel Smith MP on whose land the Reformatory School was founded.

THE EARLY HISTORY OF THE SCHOOL

The nineteenth century was an era of both enormous material progress and social advance. It was a time of Empire, the Industrial Revolution and the coming of the railways, coupled with a general higher standard of living in Britain. However at the other end of the spectrum, the poverty, the crime and the overcrowding were grim and out of this grew a need to educate nationally and to reform the penal system. In Britain institutional and charitable care has had a long tradition through the centuries (for instance Christ's Hospital was founded by the City of London in 1552 and is just one of many schools formed in the wake of the dissolution of the monasteries) and by the middle of the 19th century major advances made by several Acts of Parliament caught public awareness and their social responsibility. One of these was the Reformatory Act of 1857 that provided for young offenders under the age of twenty to be sent to a Reformatory School for up to five years instead of prison.

As a result, Reformatory Schools were swiftly set up in many parts of the country. Locally "*a requisition of Magistrates of the County of Hertford was sent to the Lord Lieutenant, the Earl of Verulam, requesting him to convene a meeting to consider the desirability of establishing a Reformatory School for the better training of Juvenile Offenders in the County*". A public meeting (as recorded in a pamphlet entitled 'A County Meeting'*)* was held at the Shire Hall, Hertford on Saturday 30th May 1857 and amongst those present were The Marquess of Salisbury, CW Puller MP, Abel Smith (the younger), Robert Hanbury (the elder), Robert Dimsdale, Charles Dimsdale, GS Thornton, MH Gosselin and the Rev. Sydney Turner, Inspector of Reformatory Schools.

The Earl of Verulam, in opening the proceedings said '*there were many questions of great social importance at the present time ... the necessity of providing suitable dwellings for the increasing population was of first importance ... and there was no doubt that a great number of poor boys and girls were driven into crime by the squalor and misery of their wretched abodes ... prevention, it was said was better than cure and one of the best ways of preventing juvenile crime was to provide the poor with better dwellings ... and a Reformatory in this county would induce them to become honest and respectable members of society ...*'

The Marquess of Salisbury moved the first resolution '*that it is desirable to establish a reformatory school for the better training of juvenile offenders for the County of Hertford, to be supported by voluntary contributions, aided by the Government allowance offered under the provisions of the Act of Parliament, 17 and 18 Vict.cap.86 and further assisted by the Minister of the Committee* of Council on Education dated January 2nd 1856'. The Marquess in his speech said that in foreign countries Reformatory Institutions had been in existence for some time and found to have been very beneficial. In Britain more difficulties were encountered than in the more despotic continental countries, for here it was found necessary in all bills passed on the subject to insist on the conviction of the offender ... and there were a number of children who, more by the fault of their parents than their own, were thrown on the world and condemned to a life of profligacy and crime ... the object of the Reformatory was to give such children a place of refuge and the opportunity to become honest members of society.

The Rev. Sydney Turner (often referred to as the father of reformatory institutions) seconded the resolution and furnished the meeting with details of his own experience: Since the virtual cessation of the transportation system to the colonies there had to be some way to keep people out of prison. He knew of no way of cutting off the supply except by preventative education- reformatory treatment at the earliest and most impressionable age ... they all felt it was better to have bees in their gardens, not wasps ... He said he had been successful with eight or nine out of every ten boys who had been through his hands. Annual expense for each boy was not more than £22-£23. The Government allowed £18 a head per year and an annual grant of 30-40 shillings per head was paid by the Privy Council if the education of the school was approved by the Inspector. Voluntary contributions would be needed for the shortfall but less the profit from the boys' labour, if any. He also said that the success of the school depended on the man who was head of it. Three qualifications were essential. He must be a man of religion, of good sense and of a practical industrial turn.

But where to build this school? Mr Puller told the meeting that one of the greatest difficulties in the way of founding an institution in the county was obtaining a suitable site for it. Abel Smith Senior had offered land and to erect buildings and let them at a reasonable rental. He said that very few gentlemen would want the reformatory on their own land but one of the most valuable of English institutions was the active and practical interest taken by men of education and Mr Abel Smith would find himself repaid in satisfaction with the results.

Mr Puller proposed *'that the offer of Mr Abel Smith to erect a suitable building and let it, together with a sufficient quantity of land for the purposes of such a school, be grateful accepted'.*

Robert Hanbury seconded this proposal and expressed his warm interest in the movement. Donations were solicited for providing furniture, meeting the initial expenses and for annual subscriptions in order to realise an annual income of £250. CW Puller MP accepted the role of Treasurer.

The Lord Lieutenant concluded the meeting by saying that '*the best thanks of the meeting be given to Mr Abel Smith for so liberally providing for the establishing of the School*'.

THE LAND

The land offered was part of Crouchfield Farm and the meeting was told that the tenant Mr Brandram would take an active interest in the management. To place Crouchfield in its historical and geographic position, the land was a small farm in the Rib Valley. The Domesday Book records that 'Hugo de Bellcampo' held extensive lands in Bengeo but the land most likely became part of Temple Chelsing owned by the Knights Templar until the Order's closure in 1312. Their wealthy commanderies (of which there were several in Hertfordshire and Essex) were granted by Edward II to the Knights of St. John of Jerusalem who held them until the Dissolution of the Monasteries in 1539. Henry VIII granted Temple Chelsing to his Knight of the Privy Council, Sir Ralph Sadleir of Standon in 1541. He died in 1587 and by c1595 Sir Robert Boteler of nearby Watton Woodhall had acquired the property. The Botelers also purchased the adjoining Sacombe estate and in

Potato picking at Great Munden, 1950

time both were bequeathed to Jane Boteler and her husband John, Baron Belasyse of Worlaby, a gallant Royalist. He fought bravely for Charles I but by supporting the King financially he was forced to sell to Sir John Gore. However by 1688 Sir Thomas Rolt, formerly President of the East India Company was the owner. Sir Thomas's descendant Mary, who married Timothy Caswell MP in 1762, came in to the property in 1774. Their son, George Caswell gambled away his fortune so the majority of the estate was sold to Samuel Smith of Watton Woodhall in 1825. Crouchfield (Crouchefed) is mentioned in a document dated September 29th 1343 when Walter Attewell granted 20 acres to Robert de Epecombe so some lands along the Rib Valley may have become alienated or sublet after the Templars' demise. Over the centuries parcels of land changed hands and as a result, Samuel Smith's eldest son Abel Smith MP extended his property by purchasing former Knights Templar ground along the west bank of the River Rib to Wadesmill. These included the Rennesley, Rickneys and Crouchfield farms, Chapmore End and Paynes Hall. Unfortunately, sale of land was necessary in the 20th century so little remains of those 19th century acquisitions still in Abel Smith family ownership.

THE SCHOOL IS BUILT

Mr Abel Smith commissioned the prolific and eminent architect and surveyor Thomas Smith of Hertford (1798-1875) to draw up plans for the school that was built by Walter Hitch of Ware. Unfortunately no plans are extant or the style known except it was built in quadrangular form and cost £1,575.00 to build and equip. The required furniture and fittings were planned and manufactured. The farmer Mr Brandram relinquished part of his tenancy of Crouchfield and instead took a lease of nearby Paynes Hall and Chapmore End Farm totalling 225 acres in 1865 from Abel Smith.
 The lease for Crouchfield was drawn up by the parties for 21 years at £115.10.0 per annum for 21 acres, 1 rod and 11 perches and is finely written on vellum-

> "This indenture made the second day of March in the year of our Lord 1858 between Abel Smith the elder of Woodhall Park in the parish of Watton-at-Stone in the county of Hertford, Esq of one part ... and Robert Hanbury of Poles ... Abel Smith the younger of Watton House ... The Rev. Charles Findlay Bayliff Rector of Albury ... The Rev. Charles Deedes Vicar of Bengeo ... and John Baptist Brandram of Bengeo farmer here in after called the lefsees of the other part ... a lease for the purposes of a Reformatory School for juvenile offenders ... the mefsuage and buildings have been

recently erected by Abel Smith the elder for that purpose by Agreement with the said lessees ... And also will at all times during the said term well and sufficiently repair amend paint cleanse and keep in good and sufficient repair and condition ... and also hedges ditches fences walls drains gutters fixtures and other appurtances belonging to the said premises ... and also will during the said term insure and keep insured the said mefsuage and Buildings against damage by fire in the sum of one thousand pounds at the least in the Sun Fire Office or in some other public office for Insurance in London or in Westminster to be appointed by the said Abel Smith. And also will at all times during this demise use manure and manage the said demised lands in a good and husbandlike manner ..."

"*The schedule above* referred to *Scullery and Bakehouse-* All the shelves in the Scullery and Bakehouse, plate rack, sink, cast iron oven door. *Larder-* meat rail slate shelves and Bearers, Deal shelves. *Kitchen-* meat hooks and screws, a large dresser with shelves, Two Storerooms, Range of dwarf closets and shelves. *Masters Sitting room-* Dwarf closets on each side of fireplace. *Day Room-* Hat pegs. *Washhouse and Laundry-* all the fittings and utensils, Six oak clothes posts with socket plugs in the drying ground. *Lavatory-* Slate bath lined with lead, slate washbasins with lead wastes, traps and pipes, large slate cistern. *Cells-* Solid oak blocks for seat, Reclining boards. *Tool House-* Shoe closet, Brackets, Knife Board, Box. *Pig Sties-* Slate wash cisterns. *Masters Bedroom-* Five wardrobes filled with drawers and shelves. *On Landing near Sick room-* Large Clothes closet. *Water Closet-* enclosure, seat ventilation, steps, landing and sash. *Cistern-* Cistern in roof and works connected therewith. *Roller Blinds-* eighteen Windsor Blind rollers and laths. *Tablet-* Tablet and inscription. *Well-* Oak Beam stages in well for lifting pump, stout slate covering to well, Oak Curb and Inch Oak Floor. *Covers-* fifty six movable Air brick covers with knobs. *Bars-* Guard Bars to all windows throughout the house. *Manure Pump-* A Manure Pump. *Scrapers-* six Scrapers of Iron. *Pump-* Engine Pump and Water Service to Cisterns, water closet and kitchens and Laundry and other parts of the building. *Stoves-* The Kitchen range with Oven, Boiler and Water supply, an ironing Store and all other stores throughout the Building. *Copper-* A large Copper. *Bells-* The entrance Bell, two Bells for the Cells, a turret Bell with strong framed Iron Carriage. *Furniture-* The Furniture throughout the house."

Abel Smith.
Signed Sealed and Delivered by the within named in the presence of
William Jefson

G. Gray, HM Inspector of Prisons approved the establishment by document dated 10th day of November 1857 in the twenty first year of Her Majesty's reign *'I hereby certify that the Herts Reformatory School at Bengeo, near Ware, the conditions and regulations of which have been examined ... and appears to my satisfaction, to be useful and efficient for its purpose and fit to be a Reformatory School under the provision of the Statute 17th and 18th Victoria Cap 86'*

Abel Smith (the elder) died in 1859. There is an agreement dated August 1893 signed by Abel Smith MP (his eldest son) allowing the trustees to carry out improvements, additions and alterations. Abel Smith MP died in 1898 and his son Colonel Abel Henry Smith MP (who became Chairman of the Management Committee) signed an agreement dated July 1900 granting permission for building a dining room, workshop and a dormitory above. Both agreements were drawn up by Messrs Sworder Longmore of Hertford and signed by all the then trustees. The original lease was held over until 1904 when Abel Henry Smith sold the site to the School. In 1971 at the time of the transfer of the School from the Herts Training School to Hertfordshire County Council, the Director of Social Services approached Thomas Abel Smith to ask if he would relinquish any possible claim to the property; he agreed to the request and this gave HCC full legal ownership of the entire Crouchfield site.

Robert Hanbury of Poles, Ware with his eldest son also Robert and with the generous help of friends had already built the Boys' Refuge on Commercial Street, Whitechapel, opened in July 1853 by the Earl of Shaftsbury as an institution for boys without convictions, *'who were destitute of parental care, control, and instruction, ready to fall prey to every temptation'*. Father and son both worked tirelessly for the needy and were able to offer first hand experience and over the years the Refuge Union retained a link with the Herts Reformatory School.

Work on the new school progressed swiftly and for the first year a Minute Book records regular meetings of the managers. Rules for the application of management were drawn up, staffing and punishments discussed in great detail. Dietary lists (amended several times over the year) with summer and winter timetables for the boys were carefully recorded. They ordered school books, account books, register books and other necessary equipment. The Boys' clothes and shoes were to be made locally so there were orders for corduroy, lining, shirting and smock and £2.0.0 was estimated to clothe a big boy. Equipment for the farm and garden was ordered too. At each meeting the list of subscribers was recorded for that month. An annual meeting of subscribers was held in February 1859 with the Right Hon.WF Cowper in the chair. The meeting was carried nem com that the "Managing Committee as well as the Treasurer and the Auditor be requested to continue their services to the Institution"

Included in this Minute Book are some thoughts for the aims of the School and begins *'The boys are to be managed and generally treated with as much similarity to a private family as circumstances will permit. The School is to be not merely a place of refuge from contamination in which you are compelled to remain, but a home to which you may become attached ...'*

THE SCHOOL OPENS

A Superintendent, James Kitley with excellent references from Bath Goal and his wife Sarah as Matron were appointed for £50.0.0 per annum including accommodation. A fine Admittance Book survives. How terrified or defiant these boys must have been! The first entry on December 8th 1857 is for Frederick Jeffrey aged 11 who was convicted for stealing a pair of boots to the value of one shilling the property of Robert East of Hitchin. The boy's father was a painter in Hitchin, his mother a shirtmaker, both of good character. He was 4'5½" tall and his educational state nil. The sentence was two years and his father was ordered to pay two shillings a week. On discharge the entry records that he 'appears anxious to do better, reads and writes fairly well by the end'.

Numbers rose quickly; the Hertfordshire Mercury dated September 13th 1863 reported that *'twenty three boys absconded from the Herts Reformatory having mutinied because pudding was refused them on the Sunday. The boys proceeded as far as the Ware Cemetery when the Labour Master persuaded them to return by promising that they should have the pudding. They afterwards refused to enter the reformatory and armed themselves with sticks and stones. At length a strong body of police made their appearance and the boys were overpowered. Arthur Samworth the ringleader was taken before the magistrate and committed to prison for three months'*. Another entry in the Admittance Book in 1865 was John Martin of Holborn, London, aged twelve was convicted for five years for stealing a gold pin from a shop. He was 4'3" fair and with freckles. He was of average general ability but no education. On his discharge on May 11th 1870 he was taken to Liverpool and sent to Canada where he was recommended for farm work.

The School developed well under the next Superintendant, James Fish. Religious Training was important and boys attended the new church built by Abel Smith (Senior) at Tonwell twice each Sunday. Other emphasis was on hard outdoor work with six acres under vegetables and a further fifteen acres under barley and seeds. Two hours a day were spent on education with additional time for those who were very backward. The last entry in the first Admittance Book (no 195) was in 1871 for Joseph Johnson of Hatfield Hyde, Herts. His offence was stealing £1.2.0 from the house of an old lady for which he received a three years conviction. His character was considered good on discharge. Other offences mentioned in the Book included stealing a sheet, a pocket knife, boxes of cigars, a goose, a coat, a purse containing ten shillings and two pots of jam and sentences were from two to five years depending on the crime. Numbers at this time rose to 50 boys and a set of rules was drawn up in a fine copperplate hand:

'CERTIFIED RULES and REGULATIONS of the HERTS REFORMATORY SCHOOL'

1. The School shall be called the 'Herts Reformatory School' and is situate at Bengeo in the county of Hertfordshire.
2. It is conducted by a Committee of Managers approved by the body of annual subscribers.
3. The number of inmates provided for, shall be 50.
4. The School shall be for Boys only, who from free of disease and bodily infirmary shall be admitted at the ages specified in the Reformatory Schools Act 1866.
5. Each boy shall be provided with a Separate bed and supplied with a sufficiency of suitable Clothing.
6. The Diet shall consist of wholesome food and shall be approved by her Majesty's Inspector of Reformatories, and no substantial alteration shall be made in it without previous notice to him.
7. The Secular instruction shall be in Reading, Spelling, Writing and Ciphering.
   The Religious Instruction shall be from Holy Scripture and so far as Members of the Church of England are concerned in the Book of Common Prayer, and shall comprise the doctrines and precepts of the Christian Religion. Secular and Religious Instruction shall be given daily during an average of 18 hours per week. Industrial Training shall be chiefly in Farm, Garden and House Work but also at the discretion of the Committee of Management in Fagot and Mat Making and such other Handicrafts, as may be conveniently practiced. The boys shall be occupied with Industrial Training during a yearly average of 42 hours per week, or 7 hours each Working Day.
8. Each day shall be begun and ended with Family Worship consisting of the reading of Scripture and Prayer. On Sundays the Inmates shall attend Divine Worship. Boys of the Roman Catholic Religion shall not be knowingly admitted. If in any order of Detention, it is specified that the boy is of some other religious persuasion, than the Church of England, a Minister of such religious persuasion shall be allowed to visit him at such hours of the day, as are fixed by the Secretary of State for the purpose.
9. The Superintendent shall be authorised to punish the misconduct of any boy

detained in the school. All faults and punishments shall be registered for the inspection of the Committee of Management.

10 Ordinary punishments may consist of forfeitures of rewards & privileges, reductions in quantity of food, confinement in a room or cell for not more than 3 days, & moderate personal correction. But no boy shall be deprived of more than two meals in succession. No Boy in confinement shall be allowed less than one Pound of Bread with Gruel or Water daily. But no boy shall be confined for a longer period than three days without special sanction of the Committee of Managers. NB. It is understood that no Boy shall be confined for a longer period than 14 days, and in that case of his Term of Confinement exceeding 3 days under the order of the Managers, he shall be allowed extra Diet, and sufficient intervals each day for exercise, and be visited by the Medical Officer. Offences requiring longer imprisonment shall be dealt with by Magistrates under the Act.

11 The boys shall be allowed an average of not less than fifteen hours every week for recreation, and exercise.

12 The Parents and near relations of the Boys shall be allowed to visit them once in three Months, such privilege to be forfeited by misconduct or interference with the Discipline of the School. In case a Boy is seriously ill, or is removed from the School by Licence or Legal discharge or Transfer, notice shall be sent to the Parents or nearest relatives.

13 On the Discharge of any Boy from the School he shall be provided with a sufficient outfit, according to the circumstances of the discharge and shall be placed, as far as practicable in some employment or service. If returned to relatives, the expenses shall be defrayed by the Committee.

14 The School shall be open to the Inspecting Visitors, at the discretion of the Committee of Managers.

15 The Superintendent shall keep a Journal of occurrences in the school, and Register of Admissions, Licences, Discharges etc. These books shall be laid before the Committee of Managers at their meetings.

16 A medical Officer shall be appointed to visit the school. His visits shall be entered in the Journal, and a note made of any serious case of illness.

17 In case of the sudden death of any Boy of the School, an inquest shall be held, and the circumstances of the case reported to the Inspector of Reformatories.

18 Returns of Admissions, Licences, Discharges etc. with the quarterly list of the Boys, under detention, and accounts for their maintenance shall be regularly sent to the Office of the Inspector.

19 All Books and Journals of the School shall be open to the Inspector for examination. Any Teacher employed in the School Instruction shall be

examined by him, if he thinks it necessary. Notice shall be given him of the dismissal by the Superintendent, and a yearly statement of the Receipts and Expenditure of the School showing all debts and liabilities and duly vouched, shall be sent to him in the January of each year.

20   The Superintendent, Officers & Teachers of the School shall be careful to maintain the discipline and good order of the School, and to attend to the instruction and training of the Boys in conformity with the forgoing Regulations. All Officers and Teachers responsible to the Superintendent for the fulfilment of their various duties, all of which are prescribed by him, and he is responsible to the Committee of Managers, for the maintenance of the general efficiency of the School. Every Boy under detention shall be required to obey the officers & teachers and to comply with the orders they may give, and any wilful neglect or refusal to obey or comply on the part of any Boy, shall be deemed to be an offence under the twentieth section of the Reformatory Schools Act 1866.

Signed Abel Smith, Chairman of the Committee of Managers.

The foregoing Rules and Regulations for the Management of the Herts Reformatory for Juvenile Offenders are hereby approved by me, one of Her Majesty's Principal Secretaries of State, in accordance with the provisions of the Reformatory Schools Act 1866.

Signed Henry Austin Bruce, Whitehall, February 1871.

FUNDING (reference: National Records)

In 1833, sums began to be voted by Parliament for distribution by the Treasury to voluntary educational bodies, in particular the National Society for the Education of the Poor in the Principles of the Established Church and the British and Foreign Schools Society. By 1839, a Committee of the Privy Council on Education was established to supervise the application of these sums to further public education and by 1856 the work was absorbed in to a new Education Department but controlled by the Privy Council so when the Reformatory Schools were established, regular funding was available for each offender (but subsidised by local donors). The Home Office, headed by the Home Secretary originated in 1782 with the allocation of duties between home and foreign affairs, became responsible for the overall administration of these schools with the assistance of local management committees.

In 1904 the Management Committee constituted Herts Reformatory Limited and maintenance for the boys' upkeep was charged to the local authorities responsible for the boys. Mostly boys came from other authorities (to keep them well away from home, so in turn Hertfordshire's boys went elsewhere). The 1908 Childrens' Act led the way to juvenile courts and as an alternative to prison, magistrates had powers to balance welfare and justice. In 1923 the name was altered to the Herts Training School and numbers increased to ninety and was recognised by the Home Office as an Approved School. In 1933 the School was designated a Senior School for boys aged 15-17. Throughout the years of the School, virtually every item of expenditure required authority from the Home Office so funding was always an issue as Minute Books frequently and patiently record.

THE SCHOOL MANAGEMENT COMMITTEE

A management committee was constituted at the founding of the School and continued until 1973. This dedicated committee of local men and women was self-appointing and the School Minute Books and Log Books record their names and actions. Mr Len Harding deposited the extensive school records with Hertfordshire Archives in 1974. Now there is the Data Protection Act 1998 to comply with but an attempt has been made to pick out interesting entries at random and in places staff and boys have fictitious initials to disguise their identity. Most of the leather books were purchased from Geo.Creasey. 10 Bull Plain, Hertford and are written in longhand, with parts in fine copperplate. Their regular meetings include records of the Medical Officers' registers of sickness, inspections on admission and discharge and surgery; the listing and maintenance of boys by local authorities, confirmations at Holy Trinity Church, Bengeo, the training programmes, departmental reports and HM Inspectors' Reports and recommendations. Also included are staffing, tenders for provisions, the Finance Committee and District Auditors' Reports and much else. The school years are meticulously recorded to lasting benefit.

HM Principal Secretaries of State set the number of boys permitted to enter the School. In 1901 it was eighty boys, 1909 eighty eight, 1910 one hundred, 1916 one hundred and twenty five *'during the continuance of the present war and for 3 months thereafter'* and in 1933 one hundred and ten. In 1957 the maximum was ninety three boys.

Law and Order in Britain has been a moral and social dilemma for the reformers, the police and the judiciary for a very long time. Over the years, in the case of children, reasons for detention changed from stealing a shilling or a pair of boots to the later much more serious crimes such as larceny, violence, sexual offences and malicious damage. The greatest admiration is felt for the distinguished men and women who gave so much time and talent to the management committees and by working with the Home Office and headmasters ran the Training Schools with great courage and determination for the good of young people in their care.

The 33rd Annual Report for the year 1890 is in a small printed booklet and names the Managing Committee as Abel Smith MP (Chairman), Robert Smith (Treasurer), A G Odell, Rev. J C M Mansel-Pleydell (Rector of Bengeo), E S Hanbury, J W Taylor, Lt. Col Bell, J B Brandam (Hon.Secretary) Rev. C A Burnaby, Abel Henry Smith.

Medical Officer: Dr. J T Tasker-Evans
The Parochial Clergy: Chaplains
I A Fish, Superintendent
Mr Darby, Labour Master.
Mr H M Sutton, Assistant School and Labour Master.
Bankers: London and County Bank, Hertford.

Abel Smith as Chairman wrote a lengthy report that stated the total number of admissions since 1857 was 467 boys and during the past year the average number of boys detained was 53. *'... The Committee have again the pleasure of placing on record their satisfaction with the manner in which the work of the school has been carried out by the Superintendent and Matron and the other officers during the past year. The health of the boys has been good and again the committee would devoutly express their gratitude to Almighty God for this great blessing ... and in conclusion they would ask the prayers of all who are interested in the rescue of the young from crime, that an abundant blessing may in all respects continue to rest on their labours'.*

In the section on the State of the School, the Committee reports that they 'are careful to admit none but those who are of *sound bodily health*, and capable of receiving *mental instruction and industrial training*. The school being essentially a school of industry, and the inmates being chiefly employed in farm and garden work, any *constitutional infirmities, loss of limb or eyesight, necessarily disqualifies for admission'.*

September 18th 1890- *'I have paid a visit to the Reformatory to-day, and examined the school classes. I am glad to find all going on steadily and well. The boys are in good health and spirits. There has been little serious illness, except an ordinary attack of influenza which affected the school in January and February - one boy in hospital from diseased bone.*

Fifty inmates to-day.
I went over house and premises; I found cleanliness and good order. The arrangements are suitable and convenient. The sanitary condition seems excellent, but I think the pigsties in the yard objectionable; they should be removed further off.

I am glad to find that the records of offence and punishment are of an average character...the boys are in excellent order, and readily submit to the firm but kindly rule of the establishment.

The school classes made a creditable appearance to-day. There has been steady progress throughout the school. The teacher works diligently and gets the lads on. Many come quite ignorant.

The practical training is very valuable. I was glad to learn that the boys had been diligent in the harvest field and earned a good report. The school continues to do well, and is under earnest and experienced management'

HENRY ROGERS
HM Deputy Inspector, Reformatory and Industrial Schools.
Home Office.

Note- In accordance with Mr Roger's suggestion, the Managers are about to erect new pigsties at a considerable distance from the School buildings.

The Annual Reports print several letters from former pupils living abroad (letter writing was a Home Office requirement) and the 1890 issue includes a heartening one from Canada. This boy left the School in October 1885-

Dear Sir- I now take pleasure to write a few lines to you hoping they will find you and all the boys quite well, as I am myself ... Dear Sir, I am glad I had the chance to come out to this country, and I thank you for helping me out here. You said you had little faith in me. I think you may have a little now. I am working at the first place which Mr G. got me. Sir, I like the place, and I am getting on splendidly. We have not had much snow this winter, and we are going to make sugar soon. Give my best respects to Mr D. and the Schoolmasters.

I remain- yours etc.
F.J.H.

PS Would you please send me a few potatoes and seeds.

Each Annual Report lays out the state of the School, the Inspectors' Reports and other details including the Home Office regulations. There was a winter time table, rising and washing at 6.00 am in the summer 5.30am and in the evening prayers and bed at 8.30pm. In 1898, on weekdays they had for breakfast *'8oz bread, 1 pint oatmeal porridge made with 2 oz. Meal well boiled in Water or Milk, for Dinner 7 oz Boiled Beef, Potatoes roasted and Vegetables ad lib ...'*

The early years of the 20th century

By 1900 the Managers, owing to changes by death or retirement, were recorded as:
Colonel Abel Henry Smith MP (Chairman), Mr Alfred G Odell, Mr Edmund Hanbury, Rev. Alfred W Duke (Curate at Bengeo) Chaplain and Secretary, Mr Reginald A Smith, Rev. Herbert E Selwyn (Rector of Bengeo), Mr Robert Walters, Mr J H Dugdale, Rev. Henry Brown Gold (Curate at Waterford), Mr J B Brandram and Mr T Vulliamy.

Superintendent Mr I A Fish, Matron Mrs Webber, Schoolmaster Mr F Cowley, Assistant School and Labour Master Mr W Pearman, Labour Master Mr J W Darby.

Abel Smith MP died in 1898 and the Chairmanship passed to his elder son. The Managers offered their sincere condolences to his widow who in return sent them an extract from his diary for May 30th 1857- *'the Reformatory Meeting at Hertford went off capitally and the Committee was arranged quite to our satisfaction. I feel this to be almost the happiest day I have ever spent, as it has been the attainment of an object I have so long desired and which has been deferred so often by various difficulties. I feel it to be an answer to prayer.'*

Managers looked thoroughly at all cases of boys considered for licence to leave at the end of their terms but this was only granted when family circumstances were taken in to account and suitable employment or emigration to the Colonies had been arranged. Financial support and clothing was also considered and boys were encouraged to turn to the School in times of trouble and to visit and to correspond and during the 1930s there was an Old Boys Association that met annually in London.

During 1902, further farmland and new buildings were urgently required and the Managers considered the possible purchase of the School and the land around from Colonel Abel Henry Smith who agreed to a valuation. Prolonged and complex negotiations continued with the School Managers and the Landlord's

The Chefs: Mr Harris and his assistant, c1964

Agent and Longmores, the Solicitors. Valuations of the parcels of land were offered and rejected and the Managers' questioned the Land Tax and Tithes. In December 1902, the Minutes record that *'the Inspector is pressing them to erect further buildings which they do not feel justified in doing under the present arrangements, that unless their offer is accepted they will be compelled, if the Institution is to continue, to purchase land elsewhere'.*

An independent valuation was carried out in 1903 and a compromise was at last reached. On March 9th 1904 *'the Contract to purchase the School Premises and land was sealed by the Secretary and witnessed by Mr Parker (acting Chairman) and Mr Hanbury in the presence of the Committee'.*

June 27th 1904: The Conveyance for the freehold was finally completed between Colonel Abel Henry Smith and Herts Reformatory Limited for the original 21 acres and the buildings erected and leased in 1857. Also included were parcels of land that had since been leased and the total area amounted to some 55 acres. It was decided that the deeds of the property would be deposited at the London and County Bank, Hertford for safe custody.

For some time, the Management Committee had intended to form a Company and *'Herts Reformatory Limited which was dated February 13th 1904 and issued on Tuesday 16th inst'* became a reality. A seal of the Company was designed and ordered and the Rev. A W Duke, Chaplain and Secretary of the Company was appointed and offered £100.00 per annum.

Emphasis on Religious Instruction was present throughout the years and on May 8th 1907 the Diocesan Inspector, Arthur J.Buckland wrote that *'I have much pleasure in testifying to a continuance of that careful Religious Instruction which I have found on former occasions'* and on February 18th 1918 his successor Basil JM Reay stated that *'this School is in excellent hands and very good results are obtained from unpromising material'*.

In 1911 a flagstaff was presented to the School by the Chief Inspector to celebrate the Coronation of King George V.

In 1918, the 60th Annual Report states that *'the Managers keep in touch with all who have been under their charge for three years after their discharge ... this enables them to advise and direct them ... a good proportion visit the school and great praise is given to those who are leading honest and manly lives and striving to become good citizens'*.

In 1920 and 1921 there was a requirement for more land for the training of agriculture and there was the need for staff accommodation and other buildings. As always, school budgets were tightly controlled by the Home Office which sanctioned limited spending in those austere years. Colonel Abel Henry Smith offered 19 acres, 2 rods and 9 perches, which after long negotiation was bought by the School for £850.00 in 1922. This land included the Osier Beds by the river and part of High Trees Farm at Chapmore End.

March 3rd 1921: *'The day was memorable by reason of a visit by His Royal Highness, the Duke of York. HRH was accompanied by Sir Richard Baird, Under Secretary of the Home Office ... all the members of the Management Committee were present and after Colonel Abel H Smith, the Chairman had been introduced to the Duke by Sir Richard Baird, the other members were introduced by him. A tour of the School was then made, at the conclusion of which the boys were assembled in the Drill Hall and addressed by HRH who spoke of the pleasure the visit had given him and pointed out the great opportunities the boys had of shaping their lives and fitting themselves to become the good citizens of the future. Hearty cheers greeted the speech which was renewed when the Duke informed the boys that they were to have a day's holiday in honouring his visit'*.

Many changes took place in the 1920s: in 1921 a telephone was connected, in 1923 an electric lighting plant was installed and the drainage improved. Despite funding shortages and Home Office constraints, new farm buildings and a much needed piggery were constructed. In 1923 the Herts Reformatory School was renamed the Herts Training School and the first lady members to the committee were invited. (Mrs C J Barclay of Fanshaws, Ware and Lady Pearson of Brickendonbury accepted). The School Rules were revised by one of HM Principal Secretaries of State who laid out the programme of education and training and the Superintendent became Headmaster.

In 1927, an opportunity to purchase fourteen acres of agricultural land from the Woodhall Estate at Temple Mead was proposed but the Chief Inspector was unable to recommend this because of funding; however the sale was eventually completed in November 1928 and proved beneficial to the farm.

In 1929, the 71st Annual Report records the committee as Colonel Abel Henry Smith, Rev. H. Brown Gold, Rev. H A Oliver (Rector of Bengeo), Mr Arthur F Bott, Lt. Col. J R Gilliat DSO, Mr H R Darlington, Rev. Roland Smith, Mrs C T Barclay, Lady Pearson and Mr H Swann. Rev. A W Duke was the Chaplain and Secretary.

'The House System continues to prove satisfactory. The prefects and sports captains are to be complimented upon the manner in which they have controlled their houses. A fine spirit of friendly rivalry exists ... the old boys' bedroom has been used most weekends...' this report also tells of a boy in the Carpenter's Shop who gained first prize in open competition at an exhibition of Turning in Wood, held by the Worshipful Company of Turners.

November 1930- *'The Committee of Management of the Herts Training School place on record their hearty appreciation for the work of the late Colonel Abel H Smith whose death occurred on November 10th. As Chairman of the Committee for thirty two years, he took the most lively interest in the School and was ever ready to help it with his wise counsel and practical advise. The Committee will sadly miss a good friend and able leader but thank God for having so long given them such a colleague.* This was sent to Mrs Abel Smith who responded with *'deep appreciation'*.

In early 1931, the Rev. Henry Brown Gold was proposed and elected Chairman.

June 6th 1932: A letter from the Home Office sanctioning the appointment of a new Chaplain at a salary of £26.0.0 per annum was read and it was resolved to offer the post to Rev. S M Wheeler, Rector of Stapleford. Mr C Stubbs, Manager of the Westminster Bank, Hertford was recommended to take on the role of Treasurer and to join the committee to which he accepted.

The Rev. A W Duke retired as Chaplain and Secretary after thirty five years and was heartily thanked by the Committee.

In March 1933 tradesmen supplying the School were considered and Tenders for Provisions were awarded to T Cox & Son for Groceries, Messrs G Garratt for flour, Messrs Earl Bros for meat and Messrs Coote & Warren for coals.

Home Office budgets continued to be a constraint and requirements for new buildings, repairs and extra staffing were frequently recorded in the minutes.

June 1934- a gardener was dismissed by the committee as *'evidence showed that he and his wife considered Leninism superior to Christianity and Lenin greater than Our Lord. They were actively concerned in the propagation of views favouring the overthrow of our present System of Law and the setting up of a new regime ...'* He was allowed £5 towards the cost of removing his furniture and giving up possession of his house. About this time, the Headmaster reported to the Managers that it was difficult to carry out all the necessary evening and weekend work expected of the staff (known then as Officers) and asked for some assistance.

In 1935 Mr A.Lugg was appointed Head Gardener and new houses were built for Officers and their families.

In 1936, sixty nine acres of agricultural land was purchased from Mr Chapman Walker at Chapmore End, and in 1937 a small area of Lammas Land was acquired from Bengeo Parish Council.

In 1937, a new house for the Assistant Master was considered.

In 1940, The Rev. Henry Brown Gold retired after forty years as a manager and from 1930 Chairman.

In 1944 the managers were The Rev. H J Oliver Chairman, Rev.Roland Smith, Rev. C H Brown, Mrs H B Webster, Mrs Nigel Hanbury, Mr E C Booth Manager of Barclays Bank, Hertford, Thomas Abel Smith, Lord Rushcliffe, and Arthur F Bott. The Rev. S. Bradney (Rector of Stapleford and Bramfield 1934-64) was appointed Chaplain at £30.0.0 per annum.

The latter years of the 20th century

Other managers in the 1940s and early 50s included Mrs Marc Overton, JP, Mr M D Hargreaves, Colonel C Butler, Mrs J R Smith, Mr G Swann (Chairman 1952-60), Brigadier W H Crosland, Mrs Crosland, Mr H E Melville, Mr W Vigus, Brigadier Seymour Mellor, Mr L A Speakman (Chairman 1947-52) ,Mr D Strang and Mr Miles Beevor.

The Minute Books continued to report on finance, farm, garden, welfare, staffing and absconders. A rewarding extract dated November 15th 1944 reads: *'The Farm Bailiff's report was read and considered satisfactory: milk yields being good and all stock well in health. Sugar Beet lifting would soon be completed; wheat sowing was finished and winter ploughing was proving satisfactory. MA, a farm lad had been successful in a Ploughing Match at Woodhall Park gaining first prize and his team of horses obtained first turn out prize. The boy was called to the Committee Room and congratulated by the Chairman.'*

In July 1943 there was a record number of candidates for confirmation and the services of the Chaplain were appreciated in connection with the spiritual life of the School.

In 1944 Dr.Colville of Ware was appointed Medical Officer on the resignation of Dr. Stewart at £90.00 per annum.

May 16th 1945- Sir Bertrand Watson, Chief Metropolitan Magistrate visited the School accompanied by Lady Watson. Both were very gratified with the management of the School and impressed by all they saw especially with the work of the Headmaster and Matron.

January 16th 1946- the Farm Committee reported that the milk yield was satisfactory. A nineteen month old bull had been purchased at the Reading Sale for 90 guineas as the previous bull had proved un-cooperative.

November 20th 1946- Thomas Abel Smith reported that the wheat had been threshed and the yield good and all millable … the two Suffolks [horses] driven by Newman had secured 1st prize as best turned out at the County Root Show …

Mr Swann and Mrs Overton both joined the committee in 1946 and Mr HE Melville of Bengeo in 1949. Lord Rushcliffe resigned in 1948 after serving eleven years and in 1949, Colonel JB Gilliat died after serving twenty nine years. Tributes on the deaths or to retiring Managers are carefully recorded for their unstinting loyalty to the School.

In 1949, Mrs Overton was disappointed with the state of the gardens but on July 18th 1951 she reported that 2000 lbs. of tomatoes, 3000 cucumbers and 112 lbs. each of red and black currents had been harvested.

December 19th 1951- *FC swallowed a needle. Absconded whilst at Hertford County Hospital. Committed offences and to appear at Hatfield Court* …

July 15th 1952- the Winding Up of the Company was considered by the Committee and it was agreed to ask the Home Office for a legal opinion. [there is no further mention of this item]

On September 17th 1952, Mr Speakman tendered his resignation. A tribute was given to him as an ideal Chairman, who always listened carefully to what members of the Committee had to say. At the October meeting, Mr Geoffrey Swann was elected Chairman and remained until 1960.

In November 1952 the Rev. C H Brown, Vicar of Bayford, resigned after thirteen years.

By 1956, Managers were each appointed for a month at a time as School Visitor whereby giving them greater access to the staff and boys and they were also given their own responsibilities for particular departments and these associations proved invaluable.

October 29th 1957 records that three interviews for the post of Farm Bailiff took place and Mr PI King was appointed.

March 9th 1959- eight applicants for the post of Headmaster were interviewed and the position was offered to Mr LT Harding, Deputy Headmaster of Court Lees Intermediate School, which he accepted. Miss M King, Matron of Warrington School, Staffs and formerly Assistant Matron at Herts Training School was interviewed and appointed matron.

June 16th 1959- *CR absconded. He was arrested by the Police and charged with breaking and entering 'The Woodman' at Chapmore End in the early morning of May 25th ...*

September 16th 1959- the Chairman extended the Managers' *'appreciation and gratitude to Mr and Mrs Clarke for the good work they had done as Headmaster and Matron at the Training School for nineteen years'*

October 21st 1959- the Chairman extended a warm welcome to Mr and Mrs Harding and hoped they would have happy and successful years at the School.

November 18th 1959- the Chairman referred to the sudden death of Mr R W Coates and paid tribute *'to his long and valuable service to the School, first as a very competent and skilful Woodwork Instructor and latterly as Deputy Headmaster. An honest, straightforward and simple man who must have had great influence upon many boys during his thirty four years of service. We have lost an invaluable member of Staff and the Managers a personal friend in whom they had implicit trust and confidence. His work for the Cadet Corp had been remarkable; the smartness of the boys had always merited favourable comments'.*

In January 1960- the Managers worked on a scheme for three new houses, a new kitchen, dining hall cum assembly room, roads and sewers. They were entertained to lunch at the School when Superintendent Inspector Hadley spoke informally to them about the desire for long term planning and advised them to submit their proposals as soon as possible for the Home Office to agree in principal before details could be worked out.

December 15th 1960- Miss A M Scorer GCB, Home Office Chief Inspector visited the School and *'had expressed her appreciation of the Managers' efforts on behalf of the School and said she was impressed by all that was being done in the interest of the boys and wished the School continued success'*

In April 1961 there were 98 boys in the School. That year, Managers considered opening a Working Hostel for older boys and a house in Collet Road, Ware was selected. Following agreement from the Home Office, the property was purchased and much of the adaptation was carried out by the School staff and boys.

Miss Scorer opened the Hostel on September 28th 1962 and ten boys were

The Sewing Room: Mrs Lewis, Mrs Phillips and Mrs Goodson, 1963

admitted. *'Certain press reports which were not in accordance with the facts were subsequently rectified by the Editors of the newspapers concerned'*

Plans for the new school buildings were submitted to the Home Office and agreed for the schedule of work to be drawn up. The Woodwork Department was fully occupied making furniture for the new house units and at the same time as producing items for Hertford's Methodist Church. It was agreed to name the new houses Abel Smith, Oliver and Speakman.

At this time, General Sir Frederick Pile Bt. GCB. DSO. MC was appointed a member of the Management Committee and soon undertook the difficult role of chairing the Release and Licensing sub-committee. In 1964, Canon Philip Ridsdale, Rector of Bramfield and Stapleford was appointed Chaplain on Canon Bradney's retirement.

Work on the new buildings progressed well and on September 9th 1965- the minutes record that *'The Opening Day celebrations took place on June 29th. The Chairman thanked all who had participated making particular reference to Mr and Mrs Harding. Mr Harding stated that during the two open days, 460 visitors had been entertained and that the total cost was £134'*.

A staff meeting, 1963

The Children and Young Persons Act was passed in 1969 and implemented in 1971 but by 1970, geographical allocation was introduced and there was concern over the large number of immigrants entering the School and the Headmaster was instructed to write to the Home Office. There was also concern for the growing percentage of drug addicts and extra security was required. Three rooms would be allocated for an Intensive Secure Unit.

November 11th 1970- the Chairman's Report stated that *'prior to the advent of geographical allocation, we had the opportunity to select and cull our intake. The objective being to select boys of a sufficiently high IQ to ensure our training facilities were used to the best advantage and thus justify the capital expenditure. Since geographical allocation, the high standard of entrants has dropped, and in many instances to lamentable levels. This has been responsible for considerable discouragement to Instructional Staff who have not been able to attain the pride of achievement they once enjoyed and standards have fallen in all departments'.*

In February 1971 the predicted difficulties of the unaccustomed Children's Officers visiting the School and serious concerns for the future role under the County Council were voiced by the Managers and Headmaster. It was no means certain that the School would continue but large numbers of social workers, magistrates, Cambridge post-graduates and others came to look and took up a great deal of staff time to Mr Harding's annoyance.

By November 1972 the continued uncertainty had an effect on the staff and morale was fast declining. Some of the most efficient and capable had already been lost and this reflected on the well being of the boys. There were thirty six boys in the School and ten at the Hostel. Special meetings were held to discuss the proposed transfer of the School and all it's property to the County Council and in April 1973, the Managers attempted to find a way of disposal through the Charity Commission and *'if the outcome was successful, then the Chairman should proceed immediately with negotiations with Hertfordshire County Council'* Final agreement was reached that the Charity Commission *'would be prepared to transfer the Trusteeship to Hertfordshire County Council and they will designate the use of the School, and shall on transfer, be for delinquent children or those that are homeless or in need of care'*

In October that year, the County Council wished to change the name to the Rib Valley School but the Managers suggested instead the Hertfordshire School, Chapmore End School or Crouchfield School. The latter was accepted.

On September 24th 1973 the Hostel closed and was used for a time as staff accommodation.

December 13th 1973- was the final Managers' meeting and each department gave their reports. Mr Harry Bott said that the normal autumn work on the farm was proceeding but with some difficulty, owing to staff shortages.

The Chairman thanked the Managers for their attendance, signed the statuary books and closed the meeting. Thus ended one hundred and sixteen years of the School Management Committee that had given first the Herts Reformatory and then the Training School unstinting service. The Committee resigned on December 31st.

SCHOOL LOG BOOKS AND OTHER RECORDS

Headmasters were obliged to keep Log Books, Admittance Books and other records that are an invaluable source for information and reference. The entries are a daily record of the life of the school and are far too numerous to quote but random entries give a flavour of the workings of the school through its varied history. One book is entitled 'Discharged Boys' and refers to boys who attended the Reformatory School and were then committed to prison between 1882 and 1887 for more serious crimes and it contains follow up entries showing their progress.

One example states that- *'HJ to St.Albans Prison for 6 calendar months for stealing a lamb. Aged 16 years. A downright idle fellow- always seemed to be short of brains. His family have been questioned in court, seems a confirmed criminal'.*

Another boy LG- St Albans Prison for 14 days for theft. Aged 14. *'A good boy here: and has done well since discharge: said to be a good labourer'* He joined the Royal Navy at Falmouth in 1884.

The Log Books included the arrival of boys (who were given a medical inspection, a bath and new clothes), discharges, absconders, staff appointments and leave, church attendance, baptisms, confirmations and athletics. Regular meetings with the Managers, the Home Office, the Police and the Courts were carefully recorded. Caning could be carried out for bad work, impertinence, wilful damage, disorderly behaviour, stealing, copying in school, idleness and inattention. It must be remembered that the School was open throughout the year and each department had to be fully maintained and staffed so their leave required meticulous planning. Boys who were well behaved or who had families were occasionally given home leave for a few days. To get away to the Summer Camps and the Corps Camps were a vital part of a boy's training and discipline as well a change from the usual regime.

The early years of the 20th century

Two short entries record an unexciting new century:

December 27th 1899- *twenty rabbits received for boys from E S Hanbury Esq. Poles.*

January 1st 1900- *oranges received for boys from Miss Bolt. Bleak House.* [Chapmore End]

February 16th 1915- HM Inspector's Report: *'Inmates 93 ... the industrial training consists of farm and garden work, tailoring, manual instruction and baking ... technical lessons in farm and garden are given in the School room ... the boys generally discharged a creditable knowledge of their work ... Home leave and camp holiday do much to maintain discipline- are events keenly looked forward to and form a most pleasant feature of the year's work of all the most progressive schools, among which the Herts School should certainly be numbered ...'*

December 3rd 1915- *ME absconded today. He was sent to work at 6.30am, he went to the lavatory and got over the door and ran away. 2 horses were purchased for £100 and 10 fowls@ 3/6 each and ten at 5/- ea with one cockerel.*

December 4th 1915- *ME was arrested today in Hatfield. He was brought back to the School and I gave him 12 strokes with the tawse on the bare posterior.*

December 23rd 1915- *today the boys commenced to decorate the school-room and Dining Hall ... Mr Masters of Woodhall Gardens very readily sent us a good supply of evergreens and the boys worked with a will.*

December 25th 1915- *The boys had special fare. Buns and coffee for breakfast. Roast Beef and Plum Pudding for dinner ... Mrs T. Barclay sent the boys oranges and raisins and Mrs Drake about 25 lbs of dates. The weather prevented the boys attending Church but they sung carols and entered into the spirit of Christmas. In the evening they were entertained by gramophone selections.*

September 20th 1917- The Annual prize Distribution was held: *TS was awarded a War Savings Certificate as the prize offered to the boy who had made the best progress during the year.*

June 17th 1918- *Today I found that Mr B had received many stolen articles from the boys ... and had encouraged boys to steal and I had no hesitation from dismissing him from the position instantly.*

[Many of the staff and boys suffered from the outbreak of influenza in 1918/19 but fortunately no deaths are recorded. Over the years boys died from various causes and were buried at Holy Trinity Church, Bengeo]

June 6th 1920- *The annual sports in connection with the Home Office Schools (South of England) were held at Tufnell Park- Our School was represented and won several prizes. Lady Pearson very readily lent us her motor charabanc and the Boys reflected great credit upon all concerned.*

The Quad, c1964

Herts Training School, 1965

January 4th 1921- *The new engine compression for raising water from the well was tested today* [in the centre of the quad] *and appeared to be fairly satisfactory.*
November 1925- HM Inspector's Report: *The School is in a very creditable state of efficiency. The teachers work hard and cheerfully and they have succeeded in securing from the majority of boys interest in their school tasks ... a somewhat bolder attitude towards educational experiments might be taken, suggestions have received careful consideration and some successfully adopted ...*
27th June 1930- *I regret that the boy HJ was drowned this evening whilst bathing in the River Rib.*
November 10th 1930- *our greatly esteemed Chairman, Colonel Abel Henry Smith was killed in the hunting field today.*

The latter years of the 20th century

June 1st 1941- Clothes Rationing introduced and coupons issued.
January 28th 1944- *Weekend Course at Hertford Grammar School for PE Standards. Mr Ray and 20 boys there.*
April 23rd 1944- *to Stapleford Church in the evening. 10 boys baptised.*
May 11th 1944- *The Bishop of St.Albans conducted the Annual Confirmation at Holy Trinity, Bengeo. 23 candidates presented. On May 21st the Chaplain held the first Communion Service in the Chapel at 7.30am with 57 communicants.*

February 6th 1947- *During the Dinner hour a number of boys went into the kitchen, articles stolen from cold store and a cake from the oven. Culprit eventually proved to be LA. Taken to Headmaster's office. He attempted to strike me and picked up a paper opener and tried to stab me ...*
November 5th 1947- *Mr Mattewson took a party of 10 boys from the woodworking shop to de Havillands. Messrs Elson and Jennings took the garden boys to a Nursery at Cheshunt to see a demonstration of soil sterilisation.*
January 17th 1948- *Christmas Concert repeated in the afternoon for the boys' parents. Mr CP Hill, Mrs Hanbury, Mrs Overton and seven Welfare Officers present.*
February 14th 1948- *a party of 18 boys went to a concert at the Albert Hall in the evening.*
February 24th 1948- *Farm boys to Machinery Demonstration at Sele Farm, Hertford. 3 boys working on the potato Planting machine.*
December 25th 1948- *Christmas Day. Boys to Church in the morning. Dinner*

served by staff and friends. Major Woodhouse visited in the afternoon.
September 2nd 1949- *Mr Rogers. Inspector of Schools, Jamaica visited. WD tractor ploughing without permission drove the tractor into the river. Headmaster and other staff spent the evening hauling it out. WD severely reprimanded.*
December 26th 1949- *boys to Delrow House School in the evening to attend Fancy Dress Party given by the girls. Headmaster to Holloway, Stockwell, Kingston and Hackney visiting boys' homes.*

Entries for a week in January 1950 typify the varied life of the School:
January 1st - *School went to a special performance of Bertram Mills Circus at Olympia.*
January 2nd- *A Larkin returned from home leave. Mrs Buxton returned to duty.*
January 3rd- *Mr Miller to St.Albans with LA and BC for Medical Examination. Headmaster returned from leave at 3.30pm. 1st Class boys returned from leave except MG (sick) and GH.*
January 4th- *Mr Bayliss returned to duty. Normal routine. Admitted TSP (Mx) and BVF (Surrey). Mr RA Forge, Home Office visited in the afternoon.*
January 5th- *Mr Threadgold to Holloway Prison to fetch HG, lost boy at Finsbury Park Station. HD absconded about 6.45 am and GG and TW during the morning. Mr Fish returned to duty. Later in the same day Headmaster and Mr Coates called to Ware Park where the two boys W and G had been seen. They had broken in to a caravan and taken a sporting rifle and cartridges. G fired a shot at a gamekeeper and Thorn one at a policeman. Both were arrested, taken to Ware Police Station and charged before an Occasional Court, being remanded in custody to Wormwood Scrubs. Later Headmaster spoke to the whole school.*
January 6th- *Messrs Baker and Carney returned to duty. Staff interviewed and advise given to methods of training. Mr LS Jenkins. His Majesty's Inspector visited in the afternoon. Mr and Mrs H brought their son back late at night.*
January 7th- *Licensed EJC. Informal Staff Party held in the evening.*

June 5th 1951- *A boy found bathing in the river during the morning without costume or towel and without permission. (this constitutes a serious breach of Home Office Regulations) The Assistant Farm Bailiff Mr Wharton was interviewed regarding the swimming episode as the boy was supposed to be hoeing mangolds.*
October 9th 1951- *A sow and 2 small pigs died... two Inspectors believe it is Swine Fever. Thomas Abel Smith came to the School and authorised the removal of 13 pigs to the slaughterhouse.*

October 11th 1951- *A telephone message received to say that the Ministry of Agriculture confirmed Swine Fever.*

October 14th 1951- *Mr Hyde took a load of pigs to Cambridge for slaughter. Boys spent all day on digging holes in which to bury pigs.*

In the summer of 1951 twenty one Training staff are listed- seventeen men and four women. The School's telephone number at this time was Ware 66.

February 15th 1952- *Funeral of King George VI. Special morning prayers.*

January 9th 1953- *School Pantomime was given to the staff and boys of Dr. Barnado's Home, Goldings* [at Waterford]

May 15th 1953- *The Management Committee met in the morning to interview candidates for the post of Farm Bailiff- Mr CF Pullinger appointed.*

June 2nd 1953- *Coronation Day- special programme and menu arranged. Short service at Stapleford Church. Television and Comic Sports. Mr N.Jefferies had a seat on the Victoria Memorial.*

September 1st 1953- *During breakfast, the cows which had been left in the stockyard were in the upper part of the garden ... a gate had been left open. The farm bailiff was spoken to.*

November 11th 1954- *two boys brought a key and file to headmaster stating these articles were in possession of SB. A staff meeting was held to warn all officers to take extra precautions especially with keys.*

January 29th 1955- *Parents Day. Concert and Open Day. Many boys' parents here. All staff and wives present. A special Sale of Work by female staff raised funds for camp and sports.*

June 5th 1956- *IG who was on licence from this school in 1955, was serving with the Army in Cyprus had been killed by terrorists.*

September 29th 1959- *Mr and Mrs Clarke vacate the Headmaster's House. Quarterly heights and weights taken.*

September 30th 1959- Mr and Mrs Harding move into the Headmaster's House.

October 1st 1959- *L T Harding accepts responsibility of the School as Headmaster ...*

December 15th 1959- *Mr Lugg, County Horticultural Advisor visited and advised on site for an orchard and rebuilding greenhouse. Evening films and Whist Drive for staff. Checked Fire Equipment.*

[the Headmasters' Log Books conclude in January 1960]

RECREATION AND SPORT

Sport was an important item in the life of the School and over the years there were dozens of entries in the Log Books regarding football matches, boxing and other athletics. Prizes were awarded on the annual sports day. A Hertfordshire Mercury report of September 1913 lists prizes for religious knowledge, most progress in the tailor's shop, best carpenters, best house worker, best darner and the most popular boy in the school selected by the boys (Shrubsole). A large variety of sports were run that day into which *'the boys entered with great zest and appeared to enjoy themselves* thoroughly'. The band of the Ist Battalion the Hertfordshire Regiment played selections of music during the afternoon and tea was served for the visitors. The Mayor of Hertford, Mr Frank Page presented the prizes before a large attendance that included Colonel Abel Henry Smith as chairman of the Governors. The Mayor, addressing the boys, said he *'noticed that everything done there was done in a spirit of earnestness, as if it was well worth doing and doing well ... whilst they were at that school they had every opportunity to both work and play in a hearty and happy way, and they would find if they took advantage of all that was being done for them it would be an immense value to them when they went out in to the world to earn their livelihoods ... he wanted to impress upon them the advantage of going about the world cheerfully. Some people were always grumbling and became a wearisome burden to themselves and a horrid nuisance to other people ...'* A hearty vote of thanks was accorded to the Mayor and the National Anthem was sung.

Boxing was another popular sport. The Log Books record matches and House Boxing and examples include- March 15th 1945- *House Boxing held in the evening. Lt.Colonel AJR Frentzell acted a Judge. House 3 won the shield.* March 24th 1945- *Messrs Morgan and Jennings to Chelsea Barracks with a party of boys by lorry to watch boxing.* November 27th 1959- *Interhouse Boxing held. A large number of guests enjoyed a fine evenings entertainment. Mrs Overton presented the shield and cups.*

TWO WORLD WARS and THE ARMY CADET UNIT

Some 225 old boys fought in the Great War. Their names are recorded on four illuminated sheets marked 'For King and Country- Herts Reformatory Ltd' and lists their regiments (both British and the Empire), ships and the Flying Corp. There were two Military Medals awarded- one being the Order of Merit. It is likely that many of them died.

The Managers' Minute Books and Log Books barely mention the two World Wars except to record the enlisting of staff, the difficulties of recruiting suitable replacements and occasional shortages. Women were employed and school life went on regardless. The popular Cadet Corps was formed and the Summer Camps instructive and improved boys' physique. Boys were encouraged to join the TA when they left the School. Random entries include-

August 3rd 1914- *Sergt. Impey called up on Active Service.*

September 18th 1918- *General Sir Malcolm Groves accompanied by Lt. Colonel Gripper inspected the Cadet Corps ...*

October 10th 1919- *Sir Charles Woolcombe, Inspector General of Cadets, inspected the Corp and spoke very highly of the boys smartness and efficiency.*

May 19th 1920- *The Cadet Corps in conjunction with the 1st.St.Albans and 13th Herts were received by the Bishop of St.Albans and Lord Salisbury at Hatfield Park.*

June 23rd 1920- annual *Colonel Healey made his inspection ... and said he had never inspected a smarter body of cadets.*

July 1st 1920- *The Cadet Corps including the OC and Lieuts Brakley Tayler and Fitzgerald, with Lieut.the Rev.H.Brown Gold acting as Adjutant and Mr Hazard as Master Cook went into Camp at Felixstowe today. Five boys were left behind on the farm. We found all arrangements for our convenience had been made by an advance party and we occupied seven huts and had at our disposal an officers' mess, a mess for the cadets, an orderly room and the use of the ablution room. The mornings were generally spent on the barracks square whilst in the afternoon, the boys paraded for bathing, cricket etc; the lads behaved themselves as Herts boys are expected to do ... the Chaplain ministered to the spiritual needs of both officers and boys.*

Most years between the Wars, the Corps went to St.Mary's Bay Camp, Dymchurch in Kent for up to two weeks and the boys have been described as very smart.

August 8th 1927- *All the boys 94 accompanied by the Headmaster, Matron, Principal Teacher, Assistant Schoolmaster, Farm Bailiff's Assistant and the Chaplain went into camp at Dymchurch ...*

December 1933: *the continuation of the Corps was considered. The County Cadet Unit would be asked for a grant towards the required new uniforms ...*

September 3rd 1939: *Owing to declaration of war between this country and Germany, the boys will not be going to camp this year. Progress with the trenches has been made and will now be completed with all speed.*

October 19th 1939: *Viscount Hampden accompanied by General Prentice inspected the Cadet Corp. He congratulated the boys on their smartness and efficiency.*

There are references to the building of air raid shelters and a request from the Hertfordshire Agricultural Committee for the School to lease more land and to provide boys for harvesting etc. The Managers insisted that the needs of the School must first be met.

In July 1942 the Cadet Corp camped nearby at Woodhall Park, Watton-at-Stone by invitation of Thomas Abel Smith. *This afforded a most useful opportunity to make contact with other Units in the County and to take part in training under other Officers and Instructors ... the County authorities were particularly pleased to find that the boys from an Approved School were satisfactorily taking their part with boys from residential, secondary schools and colleges. The Lord Lieutenant, Lord Bridgeman and Colonel Longmore of the War Office were amongst visitors to the Camp.*

July 27th 1943- *School to camp at Woodhall Park. Messrs Coates, Stanford, Ray and Cane accompanied the boys.*

August 12th 1944 –Mr Coates took 19 boys to Harvest Camp at Braughing.

September 20th 1944- *The Headmaster agreed that thirty boys could be made available to farmers for potato picking from October 1st. Transport would have to be provided and the boys would be ready to leave the School at 8.15am and be back at 5.00.*

Occasional home leaves were granted but subject to the danger of flying bombs.

May 8/9th 1945- *Victory in Europe. Special Programme carried out.*

July 21st 1946- Major Coates, Messrs Morgan, Hughes and Thompson with 79 boys took part in the Hertfordshire Regiment Rally at County Hall. HM The Queen present for the service and March Past.

January 23rd 1948- Major G.Kenyon inspected the Corp Company.

July 23rd 1949- *25 Cadets to Walton for Training, Recreation and outing.*

June 5th 1950- *to Isle of Wight. Hillgrove Camp.*

In August 1952 the School Unit stayed in Camp at Walton on Naze, the 1st week with units from Bedfordshire and the 2nd week Hertfordshire.

August 10th 1954- *Camp at Folkstone.*

July 27th 1958- *Messrs Coates and Reed took 47 boys to Annual Camp at Wouldham, Rochester, Kent.*

The Children and Young Persons' Act 1969

By the 1960s there were changes in attitude in meeting the needs of young people and their families. There was a movement against institutional care where offenders had been placed out of sight and mind and instead Society should be capable of finding solutions and those with special needs to stay in their own surroundings with their families. In the mid-1960s, Sir Frederick Seebohm (who by coincidence lived nearby at Chapmore End) chaired a Government Royal Commission on the organisation and provision of the personal social services. The powerful Seebohm Report was published in 1969 and led to the Children and Young Persons Act that year. In future there would be one door easily assessable to the public and this led to the Personal Social Services Department in 1971 embracing amongst other issues, the care of the elderly, mentally sick and young people in need. There would be a new era in social care and expectations ran high. Hertfordshire's population was expanding fast from new town development but unfortunately, the newly formed County Council Social Services Departments were not fully trained and equipped to carry out their demanding roles and officers struggled to fulfil the demands (and the expectations) made on them at this time of rapid change. These changes were of course throughout the country and affected every County Council.

Major changes came to the School following the Act. This allowed for Training Schools to cease being under the control of the Home Office and would in future be the responsibility of the newly formed Personal Social Services Departments of County Councils and renamed *Community Homes* whose aim was to give boys more social awareness, develop a skill with responsibility, reliability and greater self-esteem. Boys (and of course girls in their own schools) who were in need of care and control as well as punishment required understanding, sympathy and help. The 1969 Act brought to light many unresolved conflicts. There was a clash between the perceived aspects of welfare and the magistracy who with the police had their considerable powers reduced. The Social Services Departments would have greater responsibility for their own boys (with financial incentive to develop places in their own authorities). Thereafter in Hertfordshire only county lads were admitted but there were exceptions from the London Boroughs, Essex, Norfolk and Bedfordshire. Another argument for change was the perception that boys at the Training Schools who left with an industrial training (for instance agriculture) would never again use those skills in life so greater emphasis would be placed on education and literacy instead.

The transition worked reasonably smoothly but the Management Committee lost that special relationship they had had with the Home Office, it's long experience and in the latter years the outstanding support of the Chief Inspector,

*The Lord Lieutenant, Sir George Burns,
inspecting the Engineering Workshop with Mr Len Harding, 1965*

Miss Alice Bacon. In December 1973 The Managers discharged their duties and the School was fully administered from County Hall from January 1st 1974. The County Council was now responsible for the mental health and well being of these young people, many of them with little or no education, unstable in temperament and often coming from worst possible environments. Many of them probably failed at their primary and secondary schools and devoid of secure home life, it was easy to fall in to crime.

From May 1974 until March 1982 Crouchfield Community Home continued under the headship of Mr Geoffrey Mercer and is best described by him and other contemporaries whose memories are portrayed in Part II of this history. Mr Mercer recalls the shock felt by everyone when Hertfordshire County Council announced the School's closure from March 1982.

In due course Crouchfield was put up for sale and on August 2nd 1984, Hertfordshire County Council conveyed 122.94 acres or thereabouts to Stridedean Ltd of Hertford for £1,350.000. (by order of the Charity Commission dated April 11th 1984). Developers retained some of the former buildings for houses and apartments; other buildings were demolished and redeveloped, so today some one hundred and forty dwellings occupy the School site. The former agricultural land was divided and is still in use.

"The Herts Training School to the rescue" Cowbridge, Hertford 1968

PART II

TIME TO REMEMBER: SOME RECOLLECTIONS

MR BRIAN COATES (based on his memories)

Raymond William Coates came to the Herts Training School in 1924 as Senior Master. His only child Brian Coates was born there in 1927 and generously provided me with a fascinating account of the school as seen through his eyes. His father, physically and mentally a strong character had fought and been wounded in World War I, and then studied at Southampton University. His leadership skills were fully tested at the Training School where he was deeply respected and knew how to communicate with the boys. At the time the Head was Sidney Palmer and his wife was the Matron. The road to Bengeo was just a muddy track and Brian walked the mile or two to the local church school or sometimes had a lift in a horse and cart. He later attended the Hertford Grammar School. Brian's childhood was happy all though it was a strange environment for a small boy but he was sometimes allowed to play cricket and football or help on the farm. By this time there were about one hundred and ten boys. The school owned over one hundred acres most of it under production and he remembers the farm with a pair of Suffolk Punches and a pair of Shires ploughing. There was a herd of dairy cattle, pigs and chickens; and an orchard and garden producing high quality fruit and vegetables.

Other crafts and skills included cabinet making and woodwork. Furniture was made for mental homes and the Police College at Dorking and an exhibition of their work at Olympia deeply impressed the future King George VI. The boys helped in the kitchens and made bread rolls (known as dodgers). There was a tailors shop and a sewing matron. Boys worked hard to gain skills but football, cricket and billiards were encouraged as recreation. The bugle call was the communication around the school.

Another important aspect of the school was the Army Cadet Unit known as the 9th Herts Cadets and very smart they were too. Discipline was tough and there a drum and bugle band. Up until the war the whole school usually went to St.Mary's Bay Camp at Dymchurch in Kent for two weeks training. Rifles were on loan from HM Tower of London. Many boys joined the Regular Army and did well. In 1929, the School set up an Old Boys' Association and once a year there was a dinner at the YMCA in Tottenham Court Road. Occasionally former boys came back to show off their wives. Some boys did very well in life, some re-offended but on the whole the Training School was remarkably successful.

Sidney Palmer was an excellent head who retired in 1940. Brian always remembered him carrying a stick known as a spud. The new head was John Henry Clarke who remained at the school until 1959 and his wife was the Matron. They came from Pishiobury House at Sawbridgeworth which was the middle school for 11-15 year olds. Danesbury at Bengeo housed the 8-11 boys.

During the war, four pre-fabricated Raid Shelters were built by the boys with hurricane lamps for light. The boys took their turn in fire watching but fortunately there were no bombs near the school.

After the war, Raymond Coates was deputy head until his death in 1959. Brian Coates spent a distinguished working life in Local Government and lived in Hertford until his death in 2005.

MR AND MRS LEONARD HARDING
(based on Mrs Harding's memories)

Log Book October 1st 1959: *'LT Harding accepts responsibility of the School as Headmaster. Mr Coates handed the School over running smoothly. I have spoken to the whole School and interviewed a number of staff at their work. I have started to interview the boys individually ...'*

Thus Len Harding came to the Herts Training School as headmaster until 1974. He and his wife Paddy were both originally from South Wales. He made important changes to the school and oversaw the work on the new buildings. Mrs Harding, who has been a generous source of information for this history tells how her husband had been in the Navy and then on the staff at Approved Schools since 1946 as he felt that ordinary schooling was not fulfilling enough for him. They came to Hertford from Godstone which was an intermediate school.

When they arrived, there were ninety boys aged 15-17. The school was very institutional with barbed wire, barred windows, a high main gate and three long dormitories. Many changes were implemented although it meant some boys absconded, they were usually found quickly and returned. The boys wore short corduroy pants and jerkins; they were soon put into long pants because if they absconded, clothes were stolen to disguise themselves. An aim that Mr Harding had was to integrate the school further with Hertford's community and he was anxious that local people should accept the boys so for instance, he organised them to grow and care for tubs of flowers for the central reservation of Hertford's Gascogne Way for several years. In 1968, Cowbridge, in Hertford, was very badly flooded and the boys were sent for to help clear up the water and help in the houses, and at other times during snow they cleared the streets. Actions like these helped greatly and on Sundays they usually walked the mile and a half in crocodile to Holy Trinity Church, Bengeo for Morning Service. He knew that in the past, boys had helped build a village hall in Waterford, worked on neighbouring farms collecting up stones for road making, potato picking and numerous other supervised tasks.

The Hardings always had very good liaison with the Home Office. In 1959, the Home Office decided to re-develop the School and provide training facilities more suitable to the needs of the boys that were being admitted. Work began in 1960 on new house units (named Abel Smith, Oliver and Speakman after former Chairmen) each for thirty boys, with a housemother and father (with their own accommodation) and a small kitchen for late evening cocoa and biscuits. There was a tuck shop where boys could spend their earnings and for recreation there were billiard and table tennis tables and boys were allowed to smoke. Thirty boys were retained in the main block where there were brand new kitchens with stainless steel fittings, and a new dining room where all the boys had meals. A huge sports hall was built which was invaluable in the winter for games and football. There was accommodation for 120 boys with facilities that allowed for them to be trained in a socially realistic manner and the management were proud that the boys undertook much of the re-building work.

Another new aspect of the Training School planned at this time was a hostel at 17 Collett Road, Ware. This was opened by Miss AM Scorrer CBE, Chief Inspector, Home Office, Childrens' Department on September 28th 1962 for fourteen older boys who for some reason had no home to return to. The boys did most of the renovation to the house and Mrs Harding described it as a weaning-off period where they could work locally, learn to handle their wages and adjust to outside life. Ware was ideal because of its industry and the project was very successful. Two resident married couples looked after the hostel but overall charge was with Mr Harding and the Managers. The boys were encouraged to live as normal a life as possible and after a period of good work and behaviour they were released in to the community.

One of the chief purposes of Training Schools was to send the boys away with a skill so the redevelopment project included the improvement and expansion of its many training opportunities. These included the Engineering Department and a Woodwork Department where highclass work was commissioned by local firms. Building, painting and decorating were other useful skills. The farm had a milking herd of Friesian cattle and there were battery chickens (6 fresh eggs were sold for 2/6 from a machine near the main road). The five long greenhouses with water pumped from the river, were ideal for the boys to grow cucumbers, tomatoes, chrysanthemums and carnations for sale. Local hospitals were supplied and each evening a carrier came to take goods to Covent Garden and the Pig Unit had a regular contract with Walls.

Sainsburys at their Buntingford depot asked if the school might undertake trials for the growing of the then unusual red and green peppers under polythene. This the boys did successfully and then one Christmas, Sainsbury's asked if nuts could be packed. Huge sacks of nuts were delivered, which the boys carefully weighed and put into little bags. This was done in their spare time and earned money and funds for the school. Work like this increased and in time enough money was accrued to create a fine swimming pool built mostly by the boys.

The local Fire Brigade gave the school an old fire engine that the boys lovingly polished, took to exhibitions and enjoyed dressing up. The school had a good relationship with the Police who gave them old police motorbikes to strip down and cars were also reconditioned. Only cupfuls of petrol were given out but somehow boys did abscond from time to time. These machines were a great thrill for the boys and which gave them confidence and experience. In 1970, the emergency services staged a simulated air crash at the School being near both Luton and Stansted. The boys were involved amid great excitement and various 'casualties' were taken off on stretchers. A missing boy was later found tucked up in Hertford County Hospital!

In the Hardings' early days there was an independent single matron and many of the staff had been in institutions themselves but who were the backbone of the sewing room and the kitchen. Male cooks were employed but over the years it became more difficult to find and retain domestic staff; the school was remote and many of them did not have cars. Much reliance was put on the housemothers. After a time the matron left and Mrs Harding was appointed instead. She was happy to be in charge of all the ancillary staff, the cooks, the menus and ordering the food. Boys arriving at the school lost their own clothing but they were issued working clothes, evening clothes and Sunday suits to wear instead.

The official opening of the new buildings took place on June 29th 1965 in the presence of the Lord Lieutenant, Major General Sir George Burns. The Committee of Management was Thomas Abel Smith JP Chairman, MD Hargreaves JP, Mrs K. Overton JP, Mrs JR Smith, Colonel Charles Butler, Miles Beevor, Brigadier RN Hanbury, General Sir Frederick Pile, AH Lugg and CH Bott. Mr and Mrs Harding had a staff of forty four that included the deputy headmaster and schoolmaster, the instructors for the different departments, farm and garden staff, housemasters, welfare officers, maintenance staff, ancillary staff and cooks together with the Hostel staff. The Chaplain was Canon PB Ridsdale, Rector of Bramfield, Stapleford with Waterford. At this time the Managers and the Headmaster were confident that the School would continue to serve the interests that motivated the founders just over a hundred years earlier.

At the end of the sentence, a boy was licensed to leave on the Head's approval and was sent home or to his own county when the Welfare Officer took on the responsibility. The boy would be maintained and helped to find employment but if he erred he was returned to the school for reassessment.

Caning was permissible, but only by the headmaster or deputy and had to be witnessed; within a week a doctor examined the boy. All punishments were entered into a book, witnessed and signed by the doctor. Caning was infrequent but was a great deterrent and usually did the trick. Occasionally an old boy returned to the school and said 'Sir, that was the best thing you ever did when you caned me!'

The Childrens and Young Persons Act 1969 and implemented in 1971 changed the entire administration of the School from Home Office Control and the Management Committee to the County Council Social Services Departments. These changes became fully operational in January 1974 and in May that year Mr and Mrs Harding left the school and moved to Caversham, near Reading. On his retirement, Len Harding told the Hertfordshire Mercury that *'working with young delinquents is a fascinating experience, because you never find two are alike...they come from a tremendous variety of homes. Poor homes where they have been neglected and from homes with a heavy financial background where they have had everything. But you can never really pigeon-hole a boy. I never take any boy on face value- their problems are sometimes very deep rooted. They are probably the best actors and probably the best fibbers you are ever likely to meet. And this makes it fascinating'.* He also said how pleased he was when old boys visited the school, often with their wives and children and the many cards he received at Christmas. Len Harding was a co-founder of the Hertford Civic Society with David Kirby. He was also a keen Rotarian and encouraged his staff to participate in the community. He died in 1998 and Mrs Harding returned to live in Hertford.

MR GEOFFREY MERCER (based on his memories)

Geoffrey Mercer took over the headship of the newly named Crouchfield Community School in May 1974 from Len Harding. Originally from Shropshire, he had an impeccable background in teaching. He first taught in Independent Schools in the North. He then entered the approved schools service in 1963 at Tennal Harborne School in Birmingham and in 1965 went to the Kingswood Classifying School near Bristol. Boys from around the country were sent to

Kingswood for three to four weeks assessment and classification so they could be placed in the most suitable Training Schools in Kingswood's administrative area. This gave him a deep insight of the reform system and in 1967 Mr Mercer became head of the adjoining Kingswood Training School that was a School for 105 boys (which included a semi secure intensive care unit for twelve boys) so he was well prepared to take over Crouchfield. At the time he was Vice-President of the Heads' Association, a demanding role to combine with a new headship.

He told me how he arrived later the same day as the Hardings departed and was immediately thrown in the deep end by recovering some boys near Chapmore End who had absconded. It naturally took time to assess the School, the staff and the fifty boys. There were boys of 15 (below the legal school leaving age of 16) who had to be educated so he began to put a greater emphasis on the teaching and appointed two deputies. There were boys who could for instance make bread but did not know how to measure out the ingredients by being unable to read or write so the '3Rs' were encouraged and the East Anglia Certificate of Secondary Examinations introduced. Counselling and art therapy became an important part of training to improve their self-esteem. Just as important was the development and training for the staff and instructors to give them a clear sense of identity and high morale.

From 1971, a secure unit for some boys was planned but not fully executed until 1976. This was incorporated on the first floor of the main building for twelve boys. Extra staff were recruited and the unit was reasonably successful but the expenses soared. Training continued on the farm with its milking cows and pig unit. Horticulture, building and woodworking, plumbing and decorating departments continued but with more staff and fewer boys the economics were difficult. Sainsburys continued their tradition of experimental work and calabrise (then an unusual vegetable) was grown very successfully. Mr Mercer encouraged the boys to work in the community and the help was given on Civic Days. When he arrived, the majority of boys came from other authorities and the rest from within Hertfordshire. However the London Boroughs planned to save money over the next three or four years by keeping difficult children within their own boundaries but the excellence of the developing programmes at Crouchfield resulted in the admission of boys not only from within Hertfordshire but now a minority from London and the Home Counties.

The house in Collett Road closed and was used for a time as staff accommodation because by 1980 there were seventy two staff. In 1981 a budget crisis occurred as costs soared and there was a decreasing income from other authorities. As a result the County Council decided to close Crouchfield and this was announced in December that year to the staffs' dismay and sadness. The boys and staff began to move away in March 1982 with just a handful left to run down the farm and the other major departments but Mr and Mrs Mercer remained there until 1983. He told me that in his time at Crouchfield '*we ran a pretty good ship*'.

In June 1981, Sir Peter Barclay visited the School as author of the Barclay Committee Enquiry into Social Work Practice. He was deeply impressed with the work at Crouchfield and was genuinely shocked when the School closed. As a result, Mr Mercer was invited into University work and has remained very active. From 1983 he was an Advisor and Development Officer for the Childrens' Registered Planning Committee and in 1989 worked for the Open University creating a new course on working for children and young people. In 1990 he was invited to be a Fellow of the International Management Centre and became an Associate Professor in Human Resource Management and Senior Tutor. These roles enabled him to give help to others who were experiencing difficulties in their lives. Mr and Mrs Mercer live in North Hertfordshire.

MRS MERCER was at first appointed Domestic Bursar (previously the Matrons' domain) as being a qualified IMA (Institutional Management Association), but the conditions were poor and without a caring role, she resigned.

BARON LAMING of TEWIN CBE DL: Herbert Laming was Deputy Director of Hertfordshire County Social Services from 1971-1975 and Director until 1991. During the earlier years he knew Crouchfield well and had great admiration and respect for Mr and Mrs Geoffrey Mercer and the staff. He told me how well they all worked in a civilised atmosphere and on the whole there was very little trouble. He was particularly gratified that the handover from the Home Office and later the final closure of the school were both handled in a quiet constructive manner and there was no hostility. From 1991-1998 Herbert Laming was Chief Inspector, Social Services Inspectorate, Department of Health and was created a Life Peer in 1998. He has generously written the foreword to this history.

MR GEOFFREY SWANN JP: Geoffrey Swann was a School Manager from 1946, Chairman of the Finance Committee and Chairman 1952-1960. For many years a magistrate, he sat in Hertford on the Juvenile Bench and played a leading role in the Scout Movement. He tragically lost his only son in World War II but devoted much of his life to the care of young people. He lived in Bramfield and died in 1965. He was delighted, when during a visit to New Zealand in 1956, he was recognised by a former Training School boy working successfully at Wellington Docks. His family still have pieces of furniture made in the School's Woodwork Department.

MRS KATHLEEN OVERTON JP: (from notes provided by her daughter Mrs Archer)
Mrs Overton was a magistrate and Chairman of the Ware Bench from 1949 until she retired at the age of 70. She lived in Thundridge and became a School Manager in 1946. She was involved in the building works and took a particular interest in the gardening and woodworking departments. She interviewed for staff and supported the plan for the halfway house in Collett Road, Ware. Mrs Overton was also a manager at the Pishiobury and Danesbury schools as well as the girls' school Delrow House, Radlett. Mrs Overton died in 1998 after a long and very full life in public service.

MR C H BOTT MBE DL JP: Harry Bott was a Training School Manager from 1959-1973. As a qualified farmer, he joined the Farm Committee and advised the Farm Manager and his staff. He was a magistrate in Ware for twenty one years from 1965 and was in time Deputy Chairman and then Chairman of the Juvenile Court. His years at the Training School gave him an invaluable insight into the penal system and training of boys in their care. He has always remembered the farm muck heap- huge, square and superbly made! His family have a table made by the boys and there is a fine cross and chair in Benington Church. He remembers Miles Beevor from Welwyn (a former solicitor to the Great North Eastern Railway and later Chairman of the British Motor Corporation) was another outstanding Manager. Harry Bott's grandfather, Mr Arthur F. Bott was a Manager from c1919-1945. Mr Bott and his family live in Benington.

MR DENNIS BUZZARD (based on his memories)
I talked to Dennis Buzzard who was Farm Manager at Crouchfield from 1960 to 1984. He and his wife lived at the Lodge. After service in World War 11 he decided to go into farming so trained at the Royal Agricultural College, Cirencester and then became Farm Manager to the Chapman-Walkers at Chapmore End that adjoined Crouchfield. When he was appointed to the Herts Training School he had three staff comprising a cowman, a tractor driver and the pigman Anthony Joshua (who was also a good athlete). By then the farm had expanded to 200 acres with thirty milking cows, a few Galloway cattle brought from Scotland for fattening, a Large Whites pig unit of forty sows and two to three thousand chickens. Sainsburys asked the school to experiment growing calabrise and Mr Buzzard went to Heathrow to collect the seed of four varieties that was imported from the USA- probably the first ever grown in this country and now a popular and easily available vegetable! The farm also produced potatoes, red and green peppers and Italian tomatoes. When boys entered the school they had two or three weeks to decide which trade they wished to learn and farming was quite popular.

The day started early and was a tough regime for boys from urban backgrounds. When the school went into the care of the County Council and numbers declined, the farm was gradually run down and the last few years were very boring but when the school closed, Mr Buzzard remained to oversee the sale of the property. The farm implements were sold beforehand and the money placed in the newly formed Crouchfield Trust. On the whole he found the boys responded well to the regime but on one occasion a chap went crazy and attacked Mrs Buzzard with a stolen knife in the early hours of the morning; this was probably their worst moment in twenty four years loyal service to the school. Following his wife's death, Mr Buzzard retired to live in Thailand.

MR JOHN BING: John Bing, a pupil at the Herts Training School the 1950s, revisited the school after 50 years! Aged 13, in Kent, his crime was to cut down a tree and was caught by the village copper and as a result went in front of Judge Salt. He has a remarkable memory for detail and as we walked around the old school site, he told me how harsh the regime was. Up at 6.00am, they ran down to the river for a plunge with the PT master Chalkie White who toughened up the boys. Back to school for breakfast and then to the farm for the days work. Lights out at 9.00pm. He chose agriculture with around eighteen other boys. Mr Parfit was the farm manager- fair but very strict. He remembers the twelve gallon churns of milk that had to be manhandled and the cold of harvesting sugar beet by hand for Tate and Lyle. Boys were working in the pig unit and with the chickens. John remembered exactly what the buildings (or sites) were in his day- the sewing women, carpenters and painters workshops, the farm bailiff's sheds and five greenhouses. There was a notice board in the central quad showing the weekly grades (no bread pudding on Sundays for boys with poor grades!) Also sited here was the clinic and sanatorium with the Headmaster's house in the corner. There was a pole in the centre for the birch administered by Mr Coates. The 'cell' with a green iron door was used occasionally. Books? John has no recollection of reading or much indoor recreation but he enjoyed athletics and in 1954 was awarded an Oxley Memorial Certificate. Despite his three years harsh sentence, John Bing continued in agriculture and is grateful to the school for making a man of him.

MR CALVERT ROSE: His family came from Jamaica when he was a child and settled in Leytonstone, East London. Following a spot of trouble in 1975 he was sent to Redhill, Surrey for three months and then moved to Crouchfield and lived in Oliver Unit under the master David Goodall. Calvert described his life there and the rigorous training he undertook. On arrival boys were assessed (this was called Group 15) and spent time in each section in order to decide on a training skill where they had to remain for the duration of their term. He chose

45

Crash Landing! The Emergency Services Exercise, 1970

the building trade and was fortunate to be under the charge of Keith Jenkins and Ralph Phillips who were both dedicated teachers. Brickwork and plastering became his specialist skills and time was spent in the workshops but boys also worked on outside jobs and amongst these he helped build was part of the Sawbridgeworth Guides Club.

In Oliver House there were twenty five boys in dormitories of five on the top floor. There was a dining hall and a small kitchen but the cooked food was brought over from the main building by the boys on a rota. The usual day begun at 9.am when boys went to their departments and worked until noon. Lunch and back to work until 4.00. Then there were showers and a change of clothes ready for tea at 5pm. The evening was free until 9.30 bed. Each Unit had a TV, a snooker table and table tennis. There was a tuck shop and boys could smoke downstairs. There was education to fit in for a certain number of hours each week but Calvert was happiest in the workshops.

For recreation there was camping, biking, gym and football much of which was led by a master Rex Leuthwaite. In addition there were Christmas plays to look forward to and other occupations enjoyed by the boys. For small school offences there were punishments like early to bed, no snooker or pocket money. Calvert said that boys were given a chance to succeed in life and he is forever grateful to

Mr Mercer and everyone at Crouchfield who gave him that opportunity.

Boys were allowed out for occasional weekends and Calvert went to his mum in Leytonstone travelling from Hertford East Station but had to be back by 7 pm on Sunday. At the end of his term at Crouchfield, Calvert asked for a two year extension which was granted and he continued training. During this time he became apprenticed to Collins Builders Ltd of Cowbridge, Hertford but lived at the school in a flat with three other boys in Speakman House. These boys paid rent and looked after themselves as part of the preparation for the future. When he finally left Crouchfield, he moved into rooms above the Collins offices and continued to be employed by them for several years.

In each house there was a self-contained flat for the housefather and mother; Oliver House was fortunate to have Reg and Sheila Elphick who cared for Calvert Rose and remain life long friends. So much so that they are now 'grandparents' to Calvert's own children and he owes his life to them. Nowadays he works freelance, specialising in plastering and lives with his family in Ware.

MISS BERTHA KILBY: Miss Kilby ran Bramfield Post Office from 1937-1975. She recalls an occasion around 1950 when three boys with blackened faces knocked on her door one evening. They confessed that they had absconded from the school, were frightened and very hungry. She bravely let them in (and one produced a knife from down his sock!) and fed them; she telephoned the school and before long the Headmaster, John Clarke came to fetch them back: they had to run all the way (some five miles) in front of the car.

MR DAVID GOODALL writes: 'I was employed at Crouchfield between August 1973 and its closure in 1981. I held a number of roles, starting as a senior Housemaster in Abel Smith and then Oliver House. Then Assistant Principal (Care) and, for a few months, Acting Deputy Principal (Care). Prior to taking up my appointment with Hertfordshire, I worked for Oxfordshire County Council at their Thornbury House, Kidlington, Regional Assessment Centre from where I recommended a number of boys to the then Herts Training School ... the School provided a service to Local Authorities across the south east of England from Oxfordshire to East Anglia as well as to all 33 London Boroughs. There were very few local referrals, but some from the rest of the County. I was one of the last staff to leave, continuing to occupy one of the staff houses as part of the security, until the site was sold in 1985. I continued to work for the social services Department, being a member of the Training and Development team and a member of the Social Work tutor team at Stevenage College, Shephallbury site. I moved to Liverpool in 1994 to take up the position of Senior Manager of Liverpool City Council Social Services Directorate Staff Development and Training Unit'.

MR ANTHONY JOSHUA came to the Training School in 1965 and until 1975 was in charge of the Pig Unit. He and his wife and three children lived in a staff house on the Chapmore End road. He had farmed in Wales and Devon and heard of the job vacancy from Len Harding's brother in Wales. He built up the Pig Unit of Large Whites to 1500 pigs at any one time and each week a batch was sent to Walls on contract. The pigs were by this time 3-4 months old and weighed some 240-260 lbs. When boys entered the school they were given two or three weeks to decide on a training programme and if this was agriculture then another week or so to choose which section. Boys had to remain with their chosen training for the duration of their sentence although in exceptional circumstances there were changes. Mr Joshua had an average of six boys working in the Pig Unit but there were other duties in season like haymaking and potato picking.

There was purpose and discipline and for a lot of the boys the school provided a sense of responsibility and achievement. The staff also felt part of a community within a community in a tried and trusted system. During this time Mr Joshua instigated and led expeditions to Snowdonia and the Derbyshire Dales for hiking, canoeing and visiting places of interest. Another route was the sixty two mile Lyke Wake Walk from coast to coast across Yorkshire and boys received a leather badge for their jackets. He used to take about twelve boys at a time, with four staff and a house mother who arranged the catering and so on. The expeditions were for five days and after some initial groans and 'can't do it' attitude, the boys thrived and rarely attempted to abscond.

In 1975 after the change to County Council care, Mr Joshua ceased farming and joined the social work side and saw at first hand what the problems were. He became House Warden at Abel Smith House and took the toughest and most difficult boys, whilst John Pilgrim was at Speakman House and David Goodall at Oliver House. The secure unit was in the main building.

MRS FREDA JOSHUA looked after her young family in the Hardings' time but in 1974 she became School Secretary, then PA to Mr Mercer and finally was Domestic Bursar. In their spare time the Joshuas set up the popular East Herts Playbus Scheme. In addition he was a Hertfordshire Assessor for the Duke of Edinburgh Award Scheme, an Instructor for the Teachers Leaders Courses in the county and started the Bengeo Grey Hound Mountaineering Club. When Crouchfield closed, Mr Joshua went to Pishiobury School for a few months until it closed and then to the very tough Remand and Assessment Centre in the North London Borough of Islington. His final work up to 2000 was driving ambulances for Herts County Council Social Services Day Care where he greatly enjoyed driving elderly folk from around the villages to various day centres.

MR JIM SMITH knew the School between 1963-1965 as Contracts Manager for Howard Farrow, the firm that built Oliver House. He recalls the exceptionally severe winter of 1962-63 when his men were unable to work and Rex the foreman's car was stuck for three days on the road to Bengeo. Despite the harsh conditions, the boys played netball wearing only shorts! The new house was a good design for its purpose of boys' dormitory and living quarters. He had the impression that everyone at the School worked and trained well, there was no uneasiness or threats. Mr Smith lives in Bengeo and remembers the boys litter picking, grave tidying and attending Holy Trinity Church.

MRS SUSAN ALDRIDGE: 'Your letter in the Hertfordshire Mercury has interested me a great deal. While I never actually lived at the Training School, I was one of their nearest neighbours. My home was the Pumping Station just down the road. I went to Bengeo Infants School with some of the teachers' children. Mr Dunstone was woodworking master and Mr Bailes the Farm Manager. The school was run on very strange lines, I remember my parents ringing the school if they saw any absconders and they were always told they were seeing things. Then they would see cars leaving the school and driving round the lanes, at the last resort the Police would be called. The boys would try to get to the railway sidings in Waterford where they could hide in the wagons …'

MR and MRS ANDREW CHESTNUTT: Mrs Chestnutt's father was Archie Andrew whose Veterinary Practice served the Training School from after World War I until the school closed. From 1949 the practice became Andrew Chestnutt. Tessa Chestnutt remembers visits to the school with her parents as they were great friends of Raymond Coates and his wife.

MRS MAY KNIGHTS: after World War II she lived near Bengeo and remembers the boys in lorries being taken to pick up stones off the fields at neighbouring farms. Whist drives were held at the School from time to time and locals were invited (and collected by lorry). She also remembers part of the River Rib being dug out for swimming complete with a diving board. Her father Mr Suckling delivered bread to the School for Skinners. Mrs Knights still lives near Bengeo.

MRS PATRICIA GOODSON: Mrs Goodson worked in the School Laundry and Sewing Room from 1960-63 as assistant to Mrs Lewis. When boys arrived they were fitted out with clothes and she altered and repaired their garments. Boys were issued with clean clothes each Saturday and the laundry was packed into baskets and sent to Ware. She got on well with the boys who enjoyed chatting to her in the Sewing Room. The Goodsons lived at The Woodman, Chapmore End with her parents who were the Publicans; she still lives near Ware.

MRS MARY GEERING worked for the Chaseside Engineering Company and she remembers the early 1950s when cricket matches were played at the Training School and she acted as a scorer. She was entrusted with the teams' wrist watches. Mrs Geering lives in Hertford.

MRS ZILLAH DRIVER: in the 1930s her family lived in Ware Road, Hertford but they usually attended Holy Trinity Church, Bengeo and she remembers the 'naughty boys' sitting in the pews. How they must have disliked having to walk to Church in all weathers. She met Wally Clarke, the Headmaster's son through the Young Conservatives in the late 1940s and visited the School on several occasions. Mrs Driver lives in Hertford.

MRS QUEENIE NORMAN: her father Sergeant Major Staddon, Sandhurst trained was at Haileybury in charge of the Gym for at least ten years in the late 1920s. Once a week he went to the Herts Training School for sport and gym. He was highly regarded but a true disciplinarian to his children and to all his pupils.

MR JOHN COOPER of Waterford, formerly of Coopers Signs and Coachworks well remembers the boys coming into Hertford and they played football with the boys of Cowper School.

MR JOHN COSGROVE (from notes provided by his daughter Mrs Poyser) John Cosgrove taught tailoring at Netherton Training School, Northumberland and arrived at Herts Training School in 1920 and retired early in WWII. He taught tailoring thoroughly and some boys became very proficient and set up businesses of their own. Those years were stressful as the hours were long as masters worked all day and then had the evening supervision to attend to. The Cosgroves lived at the school and their four children attended Bengeo School. She remembers The Rev. Oliver who took services at Tonwell and later in Bengeo and the boys walking in crocodile. Mr Rich was Farm Bailiff at the time and boys delivered warm milk in cans around the staff houses. MR OWEN POYSER paid many a visit to the School and married Clare Cosgrove in April 1939. He worked for McMullens Brewery for some 50 years and they live in Bengeo.

MRS ALICE PAYNE worked in the kitchens for three Headmasters- Mr Clarke, Mr Harding and Mr Mercer, retiring in 1980 shortly before the School

Mrs Alice Payne with her kitchen helpers

closed. She cooked staff meals and supervised four boys at a time. The cooks worked in shifts, starting at 6.30am and she also assisted in serving boys' meals. She showed the boys discipline and received back their respect. She helped out with cooking at Collett Road as well. She remembers what fun the staff social events were, especially in the Hardings time. She and her late husband, WALTER PAYNE lived in Tonwell. He worked for Len Harding for about 15 years retiring at 65. Although a bricklayer by trade, he carried out plenty of jobs including caring for the boilers, driving, maintenance work and also supervised some of the boys. He became a useful member of staff and also helped Len Harding with Rotary. Mrs Payne's daughter Mrs Norris was an Avon Rep. who often went to sell cosmetics to the staff wives, baby sat for them and with her husband went on to become godparents to the son of the plumbing instructor, Horace Bower.

MR BRUCE SMITH was at the School from 1969-72 in charge of the Friesian Cattle Milking Unit. There were usually thirty cows in milk and he had the assistance of six boys and they used milking machines. At first he was single and then married a Hertford girl and they lived in a flat above the old Gym (Anthony Joshua was his best man). The hours were long and hard but boys usually enjoyed the work. He also looked after the school fire engine and took boys to shows and displays. After Mr Smith left, he worked for the Prison Service at Borstal near Rochester in Kent (this is said to be the origin of 'going to borstal'). He then moved to the Prison Service in Suffolk where he has, until recently, cared for their Suffolk Punch Horses at the Open Prison near Felixstowe. The Suffolks have been disbanded but one of them will be joining the McMullens Dray in Hertford.

Milking time: bringing in the cattle

APPENDICES:

The Crouchfield Trust (information supplied by Corporate Services, Hertfordshire County Council)

The Trust was established when the Crouchfield Community School was closed and sold and the funds used to set up the charity. The Crouchfield Trust was constituted on February 10th 1989 and slightly amended in 1994 with 'the object of the charity shall be the promotion of education and training of and provision of day care facilities including accommodation appropriate to their needs for children and young persons who are delinquent, neglected, ill treated and in need of care or exposed to moral danger by such means as the Trustees think fit for their advancement in life or so that their conditions of life may be improved and they may grow to full maturity as responsible adults'.

There are eleven Trustees, six of whom must be nominated by the County Council and are usually County Councillors, and the other three nominated by organisations or individuals concerned with the ideals of the Crouchfield Trust. A present Trustee told me that small grants are handed out and emphasis is put on giving vulnerable young people more self reliance and advise is given, for instance on the right approach for jobs applications and writing CVs. In 2007 the Trustees have granted a very substantial sum for the building of small scale hostels for young people and work on two pilot schemes will begin shortly. The Trust is fully supported by Hertfordshire County Council and all projects and investments are strictly monitored.

Hertfordshire Community Foundation is the umbrella organisation for charity and encourages philanthropy to address need and deprivation. The Director has told me that the Foundation is working with the European Union to provide help and support to those who face barriers to employment and money comes from the European Social Fund but must be matched. The Crouchfield Trust is a partner in the 'Key Fund' and has provided tranches of money over the last few years enabling the Hertfordshire Community Foundation to make such a strong commitment to this vital area, within the local economy.

I firmly believe that the founders of the Reformatory School in 1857 would be gratified to know that the considerable funds generated by the sale of the property in 1985 are used solely for the benefit of young people in need of education and training in Hertfordshire.

Chairman of the School Management Committee:

1857-1898   Abel Smith MP
1898-1930   Abel Henry Smith
1930-1940   Rev. Henry Brown Gold
1940-1947   Rev. HJ Oliver
1947-1952   LA Speakman
1952-1960   Geoffrey Swann
1960-1973   Thomas Abel Smith

School Heads and Matrons
(source: chiefly Kellys Directory for Hertfordshire)

1857: Superintendent: James Kitley   Matron: Mrs Sarah Kitley
1862:   ..   James Fish   ..   Mrs Sarah Fish
1874:   ..   James Fish   ..   Mrs Eliza Fish
1886:   ..   Ishmael Fish (son)   ..   Mrs Fish
1890:   ..   Ishmael Fish   ..   Mrs Webber
1917:   ..   Sidney Palmer   ..   Mrs Louie Palmer
1937: Headmaster: Sidney Palmer   ..   Mrs Louie Palmer
1940:   ..   John Clarke   ..   Mrs Clarke
1959:   ..   Leonard Harding   ..   Mrs Harding
                                                     (from 1962)
1974:   ..   Geoffrey Mercer   Domestic Bursar: Mrs Mercer
                                            and from 1978: Mrs Joshua

1982: The school closed

An appreciation to Mr Geoffrey Mercer
from Hertfordshire County Councillor, Mrs C D Everall.

Dear Mr Mercer,

The Members of the Community Homes and Assessment Centres Sub-Committee have asked me to write to you to express all their sincere appreciation for the many years of valuable service that you and your staff have rendered to our County in the successful running of Crouchfield School.

We recognise the sadness that all of you are feeling at this moment as the time draws near for the closing of Crouchfield as one of the most forward looking Community Homes in the country. It must surely be regarded as a great loss to the community, not simply to Hertfordshire, but to those parts of London that used it regularly in the past, and the fact that it is closing is no reflection upon the success of the work so ably provided, but rather to the change in our financial fortunes and possibly due to a shifting of views as to ways of containing and training the less fortunate and less stable young people in society.

Our chief concern now is that you and your staff find desirable fresh posts and happiness in the future. Changes are always difficult, particularly when the job that has to be relinquished is so satisfying and necessary and filling a great need. In the short time that I have been Chairman of this Sub-Committee I have become truly aware of the excellent work that the Crouchfield team have performed on behalf of the young people in their care so that this letter carries with it an element of sadness for all of you.

In the name of the Sub-Committee therefore, we send our genuine good wishes in the search for satisfactory job replacements to you all and our most grateful appreciation for the unreserved commitment to Crouchfield displayed by you and by all the members of your staff in these past years.

Good luck!
Yours sincerely

(signed) Diana Everall
March 18th 1982

A Prayer for the School attached to the Log Book 1914-1925 and said before Managers' meetings:

'O blessed Lord and Heavenly Father, the Fountain of Mercy and the source of all Light ... but since thou hast put it into our hearts, to desire to Minister to the necessities of the inmates of this School, make us fitting instruments for the Holy Work.
   Hallow the motives which actuate us and cause us to be influenced by a single wish to glorify thy Holy Name ... impart to us the spirit of wisdom, love, and a sound mind in our endeavours to reform the fallen ones committed to us ...
   Together with ourselves be pleased to look in favour on the Officers of this Institution. Enable them to impress for good both by precept and example the youthful charges confided to them and in seeking the good of others ... especially sow the seed of Eternal Life, we humbly pray thee, in the hearts of the boys in this School ... may they grow up to be useful and diligent members of Society ... give them to seek and find in Jesus Christ pardon for all their past sins and grace to know thee henceforth in newness of heart and life. Finally bless our present meeting'.

Key School Dates:

   1857   The Reformatory Act (March)
   1857   Meeting in Hertford to establish a Reformatory School (May)
   1857   The Herts Reformatory School opens (December)
   1904   becomes Herts Reformatory Limited
   1923   becomes Herts Training School
   1933   designated a Senior School for boys 15-17
   1933, 1963, 1969 Children and Young Persons' Acts
   1971   Implementation of the 1969 Act to transfer responsibility from the Home Office to Hertfordshire County Council and renamed the Crouchfield Community Home.
   1974   Full administration of Crouchfield Community Home by the County Council (January)
   1982   the School closes (March)

Some of the people mentioned in the early history of the School-

James. 2nd Earl of Verulam of Gorhambury, St.Albans. (1809-1895) Lord Lieutenant.
James. 2nd Marquess of Salisbury of Hatfield. (1791-1868)
Abel Smith (the elder) of Woodhall, Hertford, MP for the County of Hertford 1835-47. died 1859.
Abel Smith (the younger) of Woodhall, Hertford, MP for the County of Hertford from 1854 then MP for the Hertford Division 1885-98 (died). son of the above.
Abel Henry Smith MP for the Hertford Division 1900-1910. died 1930. son of the above.
Charles William Puller of Youngsbury, Ware MP for the County of Hertford 1857-64.
Robert Hanbury (the elder) of Poles, Ware. (1798-1884)
Rev. Charles Deedes. Vicar of Holy Trinity, Bengeo 1848-1875
Rev. Sydney Turner. Inspector of Reformatory Schools. Later Dean of Ripon. (1814-1879)
C J Dimsdale later 5th Baron Dimsdale (1801-72)
Robert Dimsdale MP for Hertford 1868-1874: later 6th Baron Dimsdale and son of the above (1828-98).
Hon.W F Cowper of Panshanger, Hertford. MP for Hertford 1835-1868
George Smith Thornton of Marden Hill, Tewin. (1806-1867)
Martin Hadsley Gosselin of Bengeo. (1813-1868)

Descendants of most of these eminent men still live in Hertfordshire.

References and acknowledgements:

'After Grace, Teeth', 1975 Dartington Social Research Unit, Devon
'Locking up Children', 1978 Dartington Social Research Unit, Devon
Communities Schools Gazette, 1974
HALS [Hertfordshire Archives and Local Studies]
Hertford Museum
Hertfordshire County Council
Hertfordshire Community Foundation
Abel Smith Archives
Hertfordshire Mercury
Hertford Oral History Group

Illustrations
By permission of HALS (Herts Training School Collection):
  The Quad, Herts Training School
  The Sewing Room, Herts Training School
  Bringing in the Cattle, Herts Training School
  The Chefs, Herts Training School
  Herts Training School to the Rescue, Cowbridge, Hertford 1968 (Hertfordshire Mercury)

Private Collections include:
  Mrs Alice Payne with her kitchen helpers
  Potato pickers at Great Munden, 1950
  Crash Landing at the Herts Training School, c1970 (Hertfordshire Mercury)
  The Lord Lieutenant Sir George Burns inspects the Engineering Workshop with Mr Len Harding, 1965 (Hertfordshire Mercury)
  Staff Meeting at the Herts Training School, 1963

  Aerial View of the Herts Training School (Aerofilms Ltd 1965: © English Heritage)
  Ordnance Survey Map: © Crown Copyright and/or database right. All Rights Reserved. Licence number 100047559.

I acknowledge with gratitude all those who have given me permission to quote from their recollections, using written or verbal material and for the use of their photographs.